Who better than Fouad Masri [...] h-
ing Muslims for Jesus Christ? I can think of no one. In this book,
Brother Fouad lets you into his world, his years of sharing his life
and love for the Lord Jesus Christ with countless Muslim men and
women. As you walk with him, you will gain confidence to obey our
Lord's commission to make disciples of all nations, including the
Muslim ones.

> DR. DAVID GARRISON, missionary, author of *A Wind in
> the House of Islam*, and executive director of Global Gates

Fouad Masri uses his unique platform to address what many of us
consider a unique audience, but in reality the religion he masterfully
addresses and counters represents one of the world's largest followings.

> JERRY PATTENGALE, founding scholar of Museum
> of the Bible (DC), university professor at Indiana
> Wesleyan University, and author of forthcoming
> book *The New Book of Christian Martyrs*

Since 1993 there has been a "voice in the wilderness" with a focused
clarion call to Christ followers. Fouad Masri has consistently called
the church to the mission of looking beyond one's personal boundaries
and biases to share the hope of Jesus with Muslims personally and
relationally. This book is unique to all other of his writings in this:
there has not in recent history been a time when the role of Jesus has
been vaguer and more misunderstood. The bottom line of what we
are called to share with Muslims, touted creatively in this writing,
is Jesus. All the cups of coffee, iftar gifts, and friendship building
are meaningless unless Christ Jesus is made real through us to our
Muslim neighbors. This book challenges the reader beyond fascina-
tion toward personalization of the gospel.

> REVEREND STEVE HELM

SHARING
JESUS
WITH MUSLIMS

SHARING JESUS

JESUS

WITH MUSLIMS

A Step-by-Step Guide

FOUAD MASRI

with STAN GUTHRIE

ZONDERVAN

Sharing Jesus with Muslims
Copyright © 2022 by Fouad Masri

Requests for information should be addressed to:
Zondervan, *3900 Sparks Dr. SE, Grand Rapids, Michigan 49546*

Zondervan titles may be purchased in bulk for educational, business, fundraising, or sales promotional use. For information, please email SpecialMarkets@Zondervan.com.

ISBN 978-0-310-09317-6 (audio)

Library of Congress Cataloging-in-Publication Data

Names: Masri, Fouad, author. | Guthrie, Stan, author.
Title: Sharing Jesus with Muslims: a step-by-step guide / Fouad Masri, Stan Guthrie.
Description: Grand Rapids: Zondervan, 2022.
Identifiers: LCCN 2022013409 (print) | LCCN 2022013410 (ebook) | ISBN 9780310093145 (paperback) | ISBN 9780310093152 (ebook)
Subjects: LCSH: Missions to Muslims. | Christianity and other religions—Islam. | Islam—Relations—Christianity. | BISAC: RELIGION / Christian Ministry / Discipleship | RELIGION / Christian Ministry / Evangelism
Classification: LCC BV2625 .M355 2022 (print) | LCC BV2625 (ebook) | DDC 266.0088/297—dc23/eng/20220518
LC record available at https://lccn.loc.gov/2022013409
LC ebook record available at https://lccn.loc.gov/2022013410

Published in association with the literary agency of Mark Sweeney & Associates, Chicago, Illinois 60611.

Cover design: Brian Bobel
Cover art: © azat1976/Getty Images; Musa Studio/Shutterstock
Interior design: Kait Lamphere

Printed in the United States of America

22 23 24 25 26 27 28 29 30 31 /TRM/ 14 13 12 11 10 9 8 7 6 5 4 3 2 1

To the Messiah Jesus,
whose message of hope is always worth sharing

To my friend Nabeel Qureshi,
whose faith is now sight

To all who follow the Messiah

Jesus is worthy!

CONTENTS

PART 3:

Conversational Apologetics

PART 4:

A Strategy for Discipleship

ACKNOWLEDGMENTS

The late Dr. Nabeel Qureshi desired that we write a book together on building transformational relationships with Muslims. Millions of Muslims are searching for hope and peace. Jesus the Savior can give what cannot be taken: peace in the heart and hope for the future. Although my friend Nabeel was not able to write due to his illness, my deep appreciation goes out to him and to all who have helped with this book, especially Stan Guthrie and the whole team at Zondervan.

Additional thanks to Crescent Project ministry teams of volunteers, interns, and staff. Your love for sharing Jesus with Muslims is contagious.

I am grateful for the support of my family throughout this writing project. You are loved and valued beyond measure.

I am amazed how the Savior Jesus changes lives. I praise his name, for he is the guiding light in this present darkness our world is going through. I praise Jesus for saving me and releasing me from hate. That salvation experience gave me a hope worth sharing with all people.

INTRODUCTION

It's 4:00 a.m. I'm waiting for sunrise. Sounds of mortar cannons and AK-47 assault rifles fill the warm night air. My country, Lebanon, which was once known as the "Switzerland of the Middle East," is being turned into rubble by rival militias. Members of my extended family on both sides of the Green Line are in danger.

This scene, repeated for me night after night as a teenager, hardened my heart to the world and to the gospel. I was filled with hate for people of all backgrounds, especially when the Palestinians killed one of my best friends, Walid.

Daily battles and bombings followed by suicide attacks and car bombs created in me a heart of hate toward all peoples, neighbors, and enemies. Death and destruction were all around me. The future looked dark, and God seemed far away.

I had been raised in a Christian home, but in that time of despair, I turned my back on the existence of God and investigated other religious traditions. My religious exploration led me to see the uniqueness of the Messiah Jesus compared with all other religious founders. The Lord Jesus's actions and sayings were vastly different from those of his contemporaries or any religious sage. The Messiah Jesus commanded his followers to love their neighbors and their enemies. He demanded repentance and confession of sins. Jesus invites all people to follow him, for he is the only Savior from sin.

I had the mental conviction that the Messiah Jesus is unique and that he is the Savior from sin, sin that enslaves all humankind. Yet my hard heart refused to repent and confess that I am a sinner in need of the Savior Jesus. The Messiah was someone I respected and loved, but I wasn't willing to repent.

One night a friend of my parents was eating dinner with his wife and four children. His youngest child, age two, had spilled his milk. My friend quickly scooped up his boy and took him to the bathroom to wash up. Right then a mortar shell blasted through the balcony door, exploding in the middle of the table. Racing back to the kitchen, my friend discovered what was left of his wife and three other children. With a plastic bag and a heavy heart, he gathered their remains and buried his family members.

When I heard this report, my conviction was confirmed: Religion and politics will not bring peace. Only a changed heart—a repentant heart—and a renewed mind will change a person. That day I went alone to a quiet place in our apartment in Beirut, and I knelt by the bed and lifted my prayer to God. I asked God to forgive me for the sin of hate and to renew my mind by the power of his Holy Spirit.

"Lord Jesus," I prayed, "when you came to earth, you healed the sick. You raised the dead. You washed the feet of your disciples. The more hate there is in Lebanon, the more I want to be a soldier of love. The more war there is in Lebanon, the more I want to be a soldier of peace. Forgive me for my sin.

Forgive me for hating Palestinians and Israelis. Change my heart and make me a new person. I want to follow you as my Savior and Lord."

Right there I committed my life to follow Christ.

It was a life-changing moment. I started to pray for the Jewish people. I started to pray for the Palestinians, most of whom are Muslims. Only the love of God can change a heart. Despite my fear, I received the beginnings of a changed outlook, one I would come to understand more deeply as I matured in faith. When you are a follower of Jesus, you don't judge people by race or religion or social status. You see them as God's creation. You remember that Jesus says, "I came that they may have life and have it abundantly" (John 10:10 ESV).

God saved me from sin, released me from guilt, and gave me a love for all people. This change is needed in the hearts of all people. Whatever our religion, race, or social status, the major issue is the sin that resides in every human heart. Only Jesus the Messiah can save us from our sin. He alone is the answer to the wars and hate surrounding—and indeed permeating—us.

For the thirty years since that prayer, I have served among Muslim people in many countries and in many settings. I have committed my life to sharing Jesus's message with them. I have trained others to reach them with the gospel, and in this book, you will learn the same basic approach. The need is just as urgent as it was during Lebanon's bloody civil war because we remain in a spiritual war against a common enemy, Satan. The Bible says that the devil has blinded the minds of unbelievers to the truth of the gospel (2 Cor. 4:4), and this includes most of the followers of Islam, one of the three major monotheistic faiths. Our calling is to fight not with bullets and bombs but with the life-giving, Spirit-empowered words of the gospel (2 Cor. 10:4)—that Jesus died and rose again, that whoever believes in him receives forgiveness of sins and eternal life (John 3:16–18; 1 Cor. 15:1–8).

The need is enormous. Millions of Muslims have never had the opportunity to hear the words of Jesus. The Bible is banned in many Muslim countries, or it simply isn't accessible. Hosting a Bible study or importing Bibles can be a crime in some Muslim-majority countries. Most have controlled media that do not allow objective reporting on Christianity or Christian teachings. It is a shame that, in our twenty-first-century age of information, millions have no access to the message and teachings of Jesus.

And for those Muslims who have heard about him, negative and false information about Jesus and Christians abounds, often told to them by their imams and religious leaders. For example, Muslims often hear, "Christians worship three gods." In many countries, Christ followers are still called *kafir*, an Arabic word meaning "blasphemer." How will Muslims give Christ a chance if they have such a distorted view of the teachings of Christianity? This book will help you respond effectively to some of these common misperceptions so that the gospel gets a fair hearing.

In the providence of God, the world is changing, and the Muslim world is not exempt. Many Muslim groups continue to claim that Islam is a peaceful religion, but there has been a crisis in Islam since the attacks of September 11, 2001. Never before had such a massive terrorist attack been televised for all to see. Nine years later, in December 2010, Arab movements of political and social change began, resulting in the collapse of political structures and the start of civil wars. Muslims across the Middle East and North Africa are now dying at the hands of other Muslims. Additionally, the refugee crisis in places like Syria and even in the heart of Europe is creating much upheaval, and many Muslims feel hopeless about the future.

Amid all the upheaval in the Muslim world, a new movement is growing. Unprecedented numbers of Muslim people groups have been turning to the Lord Jesus in recent years. Southern Baptist researcher David Garrison calls it "a wind in the house of Islam."[1] Many Muslims are looking for access to the *Injeel*, the New Testament. This movement is vigorously opposed by many Muslim leaders on talk shows and satellite television, is banned by governments and Islamic regimes, and yet is being used by God's Holy Spirit to help bring home many lost sheep.

Muslims who manage to obtain a copy of the Injeel and read it for themselves are ecstatic to learn of its principles of justice, grace, and mercy. The concept of the equality of all people in the sight of God is refreshing to Muslim refugees escaping from sectarian wars. The Bible is clear that, before God, we all need salvation, whether Muslim or non-Muslim, Sunni or Shiite, Arab or non-Arab. God loves all people!

It has been my privilege to serve among Muslims for the last thirty years. I have read the Qur'an, the holy book of Islam, in Arabic more than thirty times. I hold a master's degree in Islamic studies and have had the privilege of speaking to Muslims about the teachings of Jesus in countries across the Muslim world. Nearly thirty years ago, I founded Crescent Project to nurture transformational conversations between Christians and Muslims, and God has been faithful. I authored eleven books that bridge the gospel to the Muslim mind and heart.

In the last thirty years of ministry, so much change has taken place throughout the Muslim world. From Indonesia to Morocco, from Somalia to Kosovo, Muslims are seeking a message of hope. I have seen Muslims read the Bible and begin comparing it to the Qur'an, their religion's holy book. After reading the Bible, which speaks of God's nearness and love, many prefer it. Muslims are also comparing the lives of Jesus and Muhammad, Islam's founder. It's not surprising that a sincere comparison of Muhammad's life, captured in Islamic tradition, does not stand up to the Bible's faithful depiction of Jesus as the sinless Messiah sent by God. But whose life *could* bear such a comparison?

For these and many other reasons, God is clearly on the move among Muslims in our day. My hope is that this book will help you to get involved in meeting the needs of Muslims and obey Christ's Great Commission among them. It will inform and equip you in your role in Christ's harvest among Muslims. It will give you a solid foundation for sharing the gospel. It will give you simple, practical steps for reaching out, including pointers for opening spiritual conversations and for answering frequently asked questions.

Along the way, I'll share from my own and others' experiences of the Lord of the Harvest at work, revealing himself to Muslim students, professionals, refugees, and converts, changing their lives for eternity. At the end of each chapter, I have included a small section called "55 Seconds for Change." It is my hope that these brief applications change your perception and ignite in you a desire to take concrete action in sharing Jesus with Muslims.

Yes, God is moving among Muslims—perhaps even the precious people created in God's image who live in your community. This book will help you grow in love for Muslims, in your concern about Islam, and in confidence that Jesus Christ can and will use you to guide Muslims into his kingdom of light.

Part 1

WHY SHARE WITH MUSLIMS?

Chapter 1

JESUS'S COMMAND

---

*Then Jesus came to them and said, "All authority in
heaven and on earth has been given to me. Therefore
go and make disciples of all nations, baptizing them
in the name of the Father and of the Son and of the
Holy Spirit, and teaching them to obey everything
I have commanded you. And surely I am with
you always, to the very end of the age."*

—MATTHEW 28:18–20

The Great Commission of our Messiah, Jesus, was his last instruction to his beloved disciples. Jesus, the son of the Virgin Mary, the incarnate Word of God, commands one final task: to go and teach all the nations. The Messiah does not ask his disciples to subdue nations or conquer peoples. He simply says that they are to teach anyone willing to listen, anyone who wants to obey the teachings, anyone who seeks to be baptized in the name of the Father, of the Son, and of the Holy Spirit. This command is all-encompassing; it includes the world's Muslims as objects of his saving love.

This simple command turned the world upside down. The followers of Jesus multiplied rapidly and spread across the Roman Empire. The disciples obeyed Christ's command and proclaimed that a Savior had come, regardless of the religious and political landscape they were in.

KEY WORDS FROM THE
GREAT COMMISSION

A careful study of some of the key words in this command yields deeper insights that will help us as we engage our Muslim friends and neighbors in conversations about the good news of Jesus.

1. All Authority

The word translated "all" here is *pas*, which can be translated "every," "each," or "every single one." Our Messiah has received *every single authority* from the Father.

Jesus has power over political authority, social authority, spiritual authority, and natural authority. Jesus can change anything according to his will. Anyone who stands against Jesus will be removed. Jesus is building his family. God is actively involved in human affairs to help bring about the knowledge of salvation to all people.

When we share the gospel with Muslims, we aren't going on our authority but on Jesus's authority. Jesus the Messiah conquered sin, Satan, and death. Anytime we share the gospel, as he has commanded us, we are doing his will. When Jesus's followers share his teachings, we are doing this in the authority of the risen Messiah. In witnessing to Muslims who are presumed resistant to the gospel, I have seen his authority repeatedly. We can trust that Jesus will save whomsoever he wills.

The leaders of the first century rejected the Messiah Jesus. Those leaders, whether political or religious, ridiculed our Savior. No one watching the crucifixion could possibly have believed that Jesus had any authority or power. Yet Jesus prophesied about his authority and position, declaring with courage and determination that he is the cornerstone.

> Jesus looked directly at them and asked, "Then what is the meaning of that which is written:
>
> > 'The stone the builders rejected
> > has become the cornerstone'?
>
> Everyone who falls on that stone will be broken to pieces; anyone on whom it falls will be crushed." (Luke 20:17–18)

The Bible is clear that all authority is under the power of Jesus. All leaders, religious or political, will one day face judgment. They will all give an account to him.

2. Going, You Disciple

In English we read, "Therefore go and make disciples of all nations." The original Greek, however, translates, "Disciple as you go." In English we separate the verbs into *go* and *make*. In Greek, *disciple* is a verb, so "go" is implied. Better yet, *go* and *disciple* are parallel to each other—conjoined, connected.

Jesus is commanding his disciples to be disciple-makers as they go through life. Jesus does not separate the going from the disciple-making. Jesus wants us to shine where we are, to bloom where we are planted. The "going" begins by crossing the street and sometimes ends in a different country. Jesus asks us to reach out to those made in God's image all around us. Let's not ignore people in our neighborhoods, grocery stores, or workplaces. We need to understand that Muslims too are hungry to hear the words of our Savior.

As followers of the Messiah, we don't seek permission from anyone to share our faith, for our leader has commanded us to make disciples. Of course, followers of Jesus always respect the cultures and laws of different nations. We are also commanded to pray for leaders and live peaceful lives (1 Tim. 2:1–2). True followers of Christ are always a peaceful factor in any community.

In Acts 1:8 the Lord declares that we will be his witnesses in Jerusalem, Judea, Samaria, and to the ends of the earth. This is a wonderful picture of reaching people regardless of geographical boundaries. We are sent near and far. Countries and governments see borders, but the church of Jesus crosses them.

In this day, travel makes the whole planet accessible to us, so our neighbors may be far from us. Living in the United States, I have met people from Asia, Africa, and Europe and hear about their nations and cultures. God gives us the opportunity not only to fly to other countries but also to meet "the ends of the earth" right across the street.

Believers in Christ sometimes try to separate the verbs *go* and *make*. But the Greek verb structure stresses that disciplemaking is what we do daily. Our going isn't only geographic; instead, it's a personal agenda to get out of our comfort zones and reach those in our midst. The parallel verbs constrain me to see myself as a witness and reflection to the teachings of Jesus.

The disciples took this command seriously. They were relentless. Like them we must never quit and never look back.

3. All Ethnic Groups

The first disciples were Jewish by birth, but the message was to *all* people. The gospel is to all nations, regardless of race, religion, age, or education. The gospel isn't meant to stay in one group but to go to all ethnic groups.

The Greek word *panta* means "all"—an encompassing word describing all people. The stress on ethnicity, meanwhile, is a fresh insight from the Messiah. He wasn't talking about empires, such as Roman or Greek or Persian, or religious groupings, such as Hindus, Buddhists, or Shintoists. He didn't see two types of people (Jewish and gentile) but rather all ethnic groups with all their diversity. The Qur'an separates people into Muslims and *kafirs* (blasphemers). But the Messiah sees the beauty of all ethnic groups. He created them all and wants all of them to become his disciples.

What a fresh perspective Jesus gave his followers two thousand years ago! Regardless of race, religion, wealth, or even openness to the gospel, Christ's command was clear—to reach all. The disciples were not sent to judge or destroy others, but rather to teach. We aren't expected to decide who should hear the gospel. Jesus didn't give us that right or responsibility. Our command is to go and disciple *all* ethnic groups.

We are called to reach out without judging the person we are talking to. We don't know his heart or where she is on her journey to faith in Christ. This command compels us to share without judging the response.

Speaking at a conference in Michigan, I sat next to a few college students during the lunch break. I asked them if they had Muslim classmates in their university. All ten answered yes. I followed their answer with a question: Are you sharing the gospel with your classmates?

Their response was, "No, we don't, because Muslims will get upset."

I said, "You didn't share the gospel because you think Muslims will get upset—but how do you know that, when you didn't even share it?"

Tragically, these college students had already made the decision for their classmates, all based on a perception that isn't biblical. Jesus wants us to share *all* he taught us. And Jesus wants us to share with *all* ethnic groups without apprehension, for he has *all* authority.

Elsewhere, Jesus gave another perspective on this command when he said there are other sheep that still need to join his flock (John 10:16). God wants his lost sheep found! Jesus the Good Shepherd wants other sheep to come and join this fold. Then there will be no more divisions, just one flock and one Shepherd!

This good news of hope is just as fresh today as it was in Jesus's day. Divides between people must be broken down, and only Christ can do that.

THE LISTENERS

The disciples knew Jesus wasn't making a request or even a suggestion. This was a *command*—a commandment to all who follow Jesus, for all times and generations. The disciples took it seriously and spread it to the ethnic groups they reached. We can do the same.

Let me take a few minutes to focus on the first people who heard the Great Commission.

In Matthew 10 we find a list of Jesus's closest disciples.

Jesus called his twelve disciples to him and gave them authority to drive out impure spirits and to heal every disease and sickness.

These are the names of the twelve apostles: first, Simon (who is called Peter) and his brother Andrew; James son of Zebedee, and his brother John; Philip and Bartholomew; Thomas and Matthew the tax collector; James son of Alphaeus, and Thaddaeus; Simon the Zealot and Judas Iscariot, who betrayed him. (Matt. 10:1–4)

In Acts 1:12–26 the apostles chose Matthias to replace Judas Iscariot, who had betrayed Jesus. Matthias had been a faithful disciple of Jesus from the beginning of his earthly ministry.

The disciples of Jesus were called personally. Most didn't possess any political or religious authority. They were commoners in a time of oppression, just trying to make a living. They held opposing political views. Matthew, a tax collector, worked for the establishment, appeased the Romans, and collected taxes from the Jewish citizens, earning their enmity. Simon the Zealot, on the other hand, was a religious fundamentalist who considered killing gentiles and traitors like Matthew an act pleasing to God.

James and John had political desires and coveted a royal seat in the kingdom to come. Peter was sometimes slow to understand the message of the Savior and lacked trust in his leader, the Messiah Jesus.

These twelve men came from mostly humble upbringings and social statuses. They were without wealth or power. So how are we to understand their courage in fulfilling Jesus's command to make disciples? What caused the change in their fearful hearts? Why did they leave their homes and go to every land and people group they could reach? Was it simply their obedience to the command?

I don't think so. The *timing* of this commandment was the dynamic factor that changed the disciples. It came to them after the resurrection. Those disciples who ran and hid rather than stand with Jesus during his suffering were transformed just a few days later after seeing the resurrected Messiah. Their master and teacher had conquered the grave and had received all authority in heaven and on earth. They were called to go boldly for the Messiah, the One who is sovereign over all the earth. They went gladly because the One who sent them promised to be with them to the end of the age.

55 Seconds for Change

My friend, the disciples were not chosen because of their ability. They were weak, but Jesus made them strong. Jesus didn't depend on *their* authority, but rather gave them *his* authority.

Would you commit today to sharing the gospel with Muslims in the name of the One with all authority? We have many resources today compared with what was available to the disciples, and all that information is empowering, but it is not enough. We must go in the authority and power of Jesus. Let us commit to go to all people, including Muslims, until all have heard.

People sometimes ask why I want to share the gospel with Muslims. They think it is hard or dangerous. I tell them that Jesus my Savior told me to. This isn't about a social agenda or a quixotic personal quest for significance. I obey out of deep conviction and respect for the One who commands me to go. You are reading this book, so I can only assume that you want to do the same.

So if this is your heart, please pray with me:

Lord Jesus, you gave your Great Commission to the apostles, but you also gave it to me. Please help me to obey. I go in your authority, not my own, trusting that you will call your own to yourself. I'm so happy that Muslims are not excluded from this call and that many of them are waiting to hear the good news of salvation by grace through faith. Thank you for dying and rising for them too. Let me be faithful to show them your love. In your glorious name. Amen.

Chapter 2

JESUS ISN'T KNOWN AMONG MUSLIMS

MINNEAPOLIS, MINNESOTA

It's 2:00 a.m., and I'm discussing my faith and the teachings of Christ with a young Sunni Muslim from Jordan. You might wonder why two Arabs are talking so early in the morning. Well, we had just shared a cup of Jordanian coffee around midnight—and who can sleep after that? Most Arabs I've met love coffee and conversations!

The young man begins by saying that Jesus, the son of the Virgin Mary, came to prepare the way for Muhammad. Jesus, he says, prayed to God facing Mecca, the holy city of Islam. He claims that although Jesus performed miracles, he wasn't as strong as the prophet of Islam, so God took him to heaven to save him from dying on the cross.

This young man, a college graduate in Jordan, ends by asking, "And what new teachings did Jesus bring?" He was suggesting that Jesus had merely reinforced teachings that had already been given.

Because I'm an Arab Christian who believes that Jesus Christ did more than simply reaffirm what had come before, my immediate reaction is to feel offended. As a follower of the Messiah, I have to ignore the offense and focus on the person.

I understand that Jesus is the incarnate Word of God, who came to open a new and better way to God by his sacrificial death on the cross and resurrection on the third day. My friend's diminishing the stature of my Savior, I reason, betrays a profound ignorance concerning the teachings and identity of Jesus. This young man is not to be blamed for his ignorance of the teachings of Jesus.

We must keep in mind that such ignorance occurs in part because, in the name of the superiority of Islam, many areas of the Muslim world make it difficult to learn about Christianity. Even today, Bible websites are blocked, and churches are monitored and controlled. Western media occasionally may point to a church building being allowed in an Islamic country. But these churches aren't allowed to baptize Muslims into the Christian faith. They aren't allowed to publicly express the teachings of Jesus. Some countries have gone so far as to order guards to question all people entering Christian worship services. They want to make sure that no Muslim citizens hear the words of Jesus.

Many imams and other Muslim religious leaders incorrectly claim that it's lawful to put such restrictions on churches because Islam came to replace Christianity. This claim is incorrect, as Arabia, where the prophet of Islam began his work, was a largely pagan area with few Christian and Jewish tribes. Islam was aimed at converting the pagans to its version of strict monotheism. Hence, Muhammad's message was not primarily for those who already believed in one God, but rather for the polytheists and idol worshipers in the region.

Despite this historical truth, Arab nations exert continual pressure on their Christian citizens, who are called *dhimmi*, a term describing them as inferior. These Christians are often made to pay *jizya*, a religious tax that is never levied against Muslims.

It's tragic that in the twenty-first century, millions are treated as inferior simply for being Christians—which, after all, is the world's largest faith. Many Muslims feel social pressure *not* to investigate the claims of Jesus because of common Muslim views of Christians and Christianity as inferior. Added to that, Christian minorities and their houses of worship are sometimes attacked and rarely protected by the local police or leadership. This adds to the stigma of Christians in Muslim communities. While police and local leaders generally protect Muslim minorities in Christian-majority countries, the reverse is not true for Christian minorities in Muslim-majority countries.

THE JESUS OF ISLAM

Paradoxically, many Muslims have great respect for Jesus. I grew up in the Middle East and heard the name *Isa bin Maryam* often. *Isa* is an Arabic name given in the Qur'an to refer to Jesus, the son of Mary. Imams, sheikhs, and other Muslim religious leaders claim to believe in the Jesus mentioned in the Bible. Some will even say they are waiting for the return of Christ to help establish Islam (and destroy those who call themselves Christians).

Jesus is mentioned in the Qur'an, which in Islamic teaching is the word of God dictated to Muhammad, and in the Hadith, which is a collection of stories on the sayings and behaviors of Muhammad, the prophet of Islam.

Yet, unlike in the Bible, Islam declares that Isa bin Maryam is only a messenger and a prophet of God—to be sure, they say he is one of the top prophets, on the level of Adam, Abraham, Moses, and David. But, they add, Muhammad is the highest prophet of them all. Islam teaches that Jesus came to prepare the way for Muhammad. Is this true? What does the Bible say about this? Who was Isa bin Maryam? Why did he come? What did he teach? What did he accomplish?

Ironically, most Muslims have not read the teachings of Jesus and have never heard of his miracles, though they are curious. Unfortunately, they often don't have access to a Bible and largely get their opinions about Jesus from Muslim sources, which came hundreds of years after his life. With great sadness I have discovered that the Jesus of popular Islam is different not only from the Jesus of the Bible but also from the Jesus of the Qur'an.

Much common Islamic belief is captured in the Hadith, a collection of stories about Muhammad's life, habits, and commands. The Hadith was created centuries after the life of Muhammad, but Islamic scholars view it as an authentic record and second in authority to the Qur'an. The Hadith records a night journey of Muhammad into seven levels of heaven, where Jesus is said to bow and worship Muhammad. Additionally, Jesus is said to claim he has been awaiting the prophet of Islam.

THE JESUS OF THE QUR'AN

The Qur'an presents quite a different picture of Jesus. The majority of Muslims today are not Arab, so they don't read or understand Arabic, the language of the Qur'an. Unfortunately, many Muslims hear only what their religious leaders tell them and have not read passages such as the following.

- Jesus, son of Mary, is the Christ (the Messiah).

  Remember when the angels proclaimed, "O Mary! Allah gives you good news of a Word from Him, his name will be the Messiah, Jesus, son of Mary; honoured in this world and the Hereafter, and he will be one of those nearest to Allah. (Qur'an 3:45)

- Mary, Jesus's mother, was a virgin.

  Mary wondered, "My Lord! How can I have a child when no man has ever touched me?" An angel replied, "So will it be. Allah creates what He wills. When He decrees a matter, He simply tells it, 'Be!' And it is!" (Qur'an 3:47)

- Jesus is a prophet.

  Say, O believers, "We believe in Allah and what has been revealed to us; and what was revealed to Abraham, Ishmael, Isaac, Jacob, and his descendants; and what was given to Moses, Jesus, and other prophets from their Lord. We make no distinction between any of them. And to Allah we all submit." (Qur'an 2:136)

  Then in the footsteps of these prophets, We sent Our messengers, and after them We sent Jesus, son of Mary, and granted him the Gospel, and instilled compassion and mercy into the hearts of his followers. As for monasticism, they made it up—We never ordained it for them—only seeking to please Allah, yet they did not even observe it strictly. So We rewarded those of them who were faithful. But most of them are rebellious. (Qur'an 57:27)

- Jesus is pure and sinless.
  He responded, "I am only a messenger from your Lord, sent to bless you with a pure son." (Qur'an 19:19)

- Jesus is the Word of God.
  O People of the Book! Do not go to extremes regarding your faith; say nothing about Allah except the truth. The Messiah, Jesus, son of Mary, was no more than a messenger of Allah and the fulfilment of His Word through Mary and a spirit created by a command from Him. So believe in Allah and His messengers and do not say, "Trinity." Stop!—for your own good. Allah is only One God. Glory be to Him! He is far above having a son! To Him belongs whatever is in the heavens and whatever is on the earth. And Allah is sufficient as a Trustee of Affairs. (Qur'an 4:171)

- Jesus would be born, die, and rise from the dead.
  Peace be upon him the day he was born, and the day of his death, and the day he will be raised back to life! (Qur'an 19:15)

In these qur'anic verses we see a major conflict with common Islamic teachings about Jesus. The Qur'an clearly says that Jesus is the Word of God (*kalimat-u-llah*) and that Jesus is the spirit of God (*ruh-u-llah*). Additionally, the Qur'an repeatedly commands Muslims to believe in the messages of Moses and Jesus. It claims that God is the source of these messages, and they are preserved in the Book of Moses (*Tawrat*) and the Book of Jesus (*Injeel*).

Entering a Starbucks one afternoon several years ago, I struck up a conversation with two Arab Muslims. One was a Palestinian medical doctor who was respectful and open to hear about Jesus. The other was a Syrian real estate agent who immediately became hostile after he found out that I was a minister of the gospel. He interrupted the conversation by stating that as a Muslim, one must "believe" in Jesus or cannot be Muslim. I inquired, "Do you read the Injeel (New Testament)?"

He answered with an emphatic no and followed it up with, "It's been corrupted and falsified!"

I asked another question: "Do you follow the teachings of Jesus?"

He responded, "No, I follow the teachings of Muhammad!"

I responded, "Sir, you believe in Jesus like I believe in Napoleon, the French dictator of old. I don't read or follow his teachings. You are doing the same with the Messiah Jesus!"

Yes, we are told that Muslims "believe in Jesus." The truth is most Muslims know little about the Jesus of the Qur'an, let alone the Jesus of the Bible. What follows are a few verses that highlight the Jesus of the Bible unknown to Islam. A more detailed discussion of Jesus, the son of Mary, is covered in chapters 16 and 17.

JESUS IN THE NEW TESTAMENT (INJEEL)

The Qur'an claims the Injeel was revealed to Jesus, much as the Qur'an was revealed to Muhammad. Yet the Injeel is hard to get and sometimes illegal in much of the Muslim world. Muslims don't know the teachings about Jesus in the Bible.

Here are some of the key ones.

Jesus, son of Mary, . . .

- is the Messiah (Matt. 1:16)
- was born of the Virgin Mary (Matt. 1:23; Luke 1:31–32)
- fulfills prophecy (Luke 2:6–7; Isa. 53:11)
- is the Son of God (Matt. 16:15–17; John 8:58; Col. 1:15)
- is Lord of creation (Matt. 14:25)
- heals the sick (Luke 17:12–14)
- raises the dead (John 11:43–44)
- existed before all creation (John 1:3)
- is the Word of God (John 1:1, 14)
- is the Lamb of God (John 1:36)
- is the way, the truth, and the life (John 14:6)
- is sinless (Heb. 4:15)
- is the High Priest (Heb. 7:24–25)
- is the perfect sacrifice (Heb. 9:13–14)
- is the healer (Matt. 4:23)
- rose from the dead (John 20:26–28; Luke 24:5–7)
- ascended to heaven (Acts 1:9)
- will return (Acts 1:11)
- will have an unmistakable second coming (Matt. 24:26–27)
- is seated at the right hand of God (Mark 16:19; Col. 3:1)
- has always existed (John 8:58)
- is the resurrection and the life (John 11:25–26)
- speaks words that come from God (Heb. 1:1–2)
- was crucified (Luke 23:33–34)
- died (John 19:30)
- was buried (John 19:40–42)

All these verses and more show the stark difference between the Jesus of the Bible and the Jesus of Islam. What a tragedy that millions of Muslims live in the conviction that they know Jesus—but have no access to his teachings. Islam teaches that the writings about Christ in the Injeel have been corrupted, but that is a discussion for another day. The writings that Christians around the world agree constitute the written word of God agree that Jesus is much more than a prophet!

55 Seconds for Change

Jesus is the Word of God mentioned in both the Qur'an and the Injeel. The time is now to share the teachings of Jesus with Muslims. Millions don't know that he said, "I came that they may have life and have it abundantly" (John 10:10 ESV).

When the topic of the Messiah Jesus comes up in conversation, talk about our Savior. Share the teachings, tell the parables, and mention the miracles he did.

Commit to sharing this Jesus, the *biblical* Jesus, so that they might experience abundant life.

If you agree, please pray this prayer with me:

Heavenly Father, you sent your only Son, Jesus, to die for the sins of the world—a world that assuredly includes Muslim men, women, boys, and girls. Many of these precious people have a distorted or incomplete understanding of the Savior. There are many reasons for this, but one certainly is that there aren't enough Christians willing to go to them and explain the truth. Please equip me with the truths of your Word and the power of your Holy Spirit. Let me be a part of the solution, to the praise and glory of Jesus Christ. In his name. Amen.

Chapter 3

TYPES OF MUSLIMS

One summer morning, on the campus of the American University of Beirut, I met two young Shia men. They were angry and said they were part of a local militia. Why were they upset? I had offered them both an Arabic Injeel. Rather than being offended myself, I asked them why they were frustrated, since, I said, the Qur'an commands respect for and belief in the Injeel, the message of Jesus.

In response, these two young men stated that the Bible has been corrupted, which is a common position in the Muslim world. I immediately responded that their comment astonished me. They had just insulted God. No one can change God's Word, I said. Rather than becoming angrier, they became curious, surprised by my answer. Not only that, one of them said he had judged the New Testament unfairly, and he was planning to read it. Both asked if they could keep the New Testaments I had offered.

Islam should not be oversimplified. Islam isn't monolithic in its practice and understanding, and neither are the people who follow it. There are many flavors of Islam, just as there are many varieties of Christianity. And even those Muslims, like the two young men at the American University, whom we may expect to fit our preconceived notions, can end up surprising us.

TWO MUSLIM SECTS

Christians seeking to share the gospel need to know more about the beliefs of their Muslim friends. We need to gather accurate information about them so that we can be most useful to our Lord—and to them. What follows is a basic introduction to the varieties of Islam and the kinds of Muslims we most often meet.

Sunni Islam

The largest sect in Islam is called Sunni, from the Arabic word *Sunna*, which means "path." Sunni Islam resulted from a major civil war among the Muslim armies concerning who should succeed Muhammad. Sunni Muslims' basic premise is that Muhammad is the model Muslim, and his path is the guide for all Muslims. The Sunna is the Arabic name given to a collection of requirements on all details of a Muslim's life. Sunni Muslims have multiple branches under the same umbrella, with cultural and religious differences.

Shia Islam

Shia is an Arabic word meaning "followers." It's the name given to the Muslims who supported Ali, the cousin of Muhammad, in his demand to be Muhammad's successor. Shia Muslims believe in divinely guided imams and the holiness of the bloodline of Muhammad. Every year Shia Muslims mourn the murder of Ali's son, Hussein, on the tenth of Muharram, the first month of the Muslim calendar. They blame Sunni Muslims.

THREE MUSLIM SUBGROUPS

Both major groups have different subgroups, each with a mix of teachings, practices, and traditions. But there is still more to know. Whenever I can, I try to place my Muslim friend in one of the following three categories. Whether Sunni or Shia, this person was raised as a Muslim, and he or she can be placed in one of these three general categories.

Cultural Muslims

The majority of Muslims today are *cultural*. Much like nominal Christians who never attend church or study the Bible, these Muslims have traditional and superficial information about their religion and the religions of others. They mix cultural norms with Islamic traditions, making it more difficult for us to evaluate their religion. They may hold misconceptions about Christianity and may be able to discuss Jesus or Christianity with an open mind. As you meet cultural Muslims, use the kinds of conversational apologetics we will discuss to win a hearing on the uniqueness of Jesus.

Devout Muslims

Other Muslims you meet practice their rituals and read their Qur'an. Many devout Muslims believe they are authorities on Islam because they practice its tenets. Whether or not this is true, be sure to show respect and talk with them straightforwardly.

I once met a Turkish man who found out I was a minister of the gospel. He immediately asked if he could speak about Islam in my congregation. I asked if he could read the Qur'an in Arabic, since Muslims consider Arabic the holy language.

He admitted that he spoke only Turkish. When I told him I've read the Qur'an in Arabic more than thirty times, I was able to have a conversation about faith with him.

Always share the gospel and be prepared to correct the misconceptions devout Muslims hold about Christianity. See chapter 13 for some of the most common misconceptions. Don't decide that just because they are devout, they aren't open to a conversation about Jesus. On the contrary, devout Muslims want to know God, and we are praying that they find the Savior Jesus.

Militant Muslims

It's a tragic fact of life that some Muslims are militant, believing they are part of a jihad against non-Muslims. As with the two men at American University, they can be angry and argumentative. But you can still win them to Christ if you approach them with a loving spirit and a lot of patience.

Always listen and ask thought-provoking questions. Focus the conversation on Jesus and his unique teachings. Many militant Muslims are thirsty for forgiveness, though they may not know it. They may be in such an angry and shameful condition that they're unable to view others clearly. Pray for God to give you wisdom. Pray for a sincere heart in the Muslim you're speaking to. Don't be afraid, for Jesus is always with you.

55 Seconds for Change

Stay focused on the authenticity of the Bible. It does not matter how devout a Muslim may be. Shine the light of Jesus, and the Lord will do the rest. God always uses conversations to open the hearts of the listeners. The words of the Bible will convict people because the spirit of God is at work. Our words are limited; God's Word is not.

God sees your heart, so regardless of your perceptions or even cultural stereotypes, take the initiative. Stay committed to share the truth in love (Eph. 4:15). Those God is calling *will* respond. As Scripture says,

> The true light, which gives light to everyone, was coming into the world. He was in the world, and the world was made through him, yet the world did not know him. He came to his own, and his own people did not receive him. But to all who did receive him, who believed in his name, he gave the right to become children of God, who were born, not of blood nor of the will of the flesh nor of the will of man, but of God. (John 1:9-13 ESV)

Chapter 4

MUSLIMS ARE IN SPIRITUAL DARKNESS

It was a beautiful day on the bustling island of Manhattan. My wife and I rented bikes and rode all the way to the 9/11 memorial. It was a somber feeling, standing there reading the names etched around the pools where the buildings once stood. A deep sadness overtook my soul as I reflected on the loss of innocent lives that day. I had heard about the possibility of such attacks when I was still in high school. Turning from my melancholy, I prayed right there for a spiritual awakening to sweep over the Muslim world, for a revival of the church around the world, and for wisdom for political leaders to create free societies.

CRISIS WITHIN ISLAM

The twenty-first century is sometimes said to have opened with the attacks of September 11, 2001. The Muslim world was stunned, even divided. Some cheered and honored Osama bin Laden with the title of Al Mansoor (the victorious); others were saddened and shocked that this act was carried out by Muslims.

Imams and Muslim countries, for their part, quickly launched a series of public relations initiatives after 9/11 to promote Islam as a peaceful religion. Muslim speakers came to churches and interfaith dialogues and spoke with news media, sharing the peacefulness of Islam. They dismissed talk of a Muslim jihad, or holy war, against America and the West. But what is the truth?

Muslim leaders often say that *jihad* does not mean "holy war," but this is only partially true. While the Arabic word itself means "to strive," in Islamic history and teachings, *jihad* is the term used for spreading Islam through force. Muhammad in AD 622 claimed that God told him to attack those who attacked him. This started what he called jihad against the kuffar and mushrikeen, with *kuffar* being unbelievers and *mushrikeen* those who make something or someone equal to God.

In the Qur'an 25:52, God commands Muhammad to declare jihad. Chapters 9 and 47 are dedicated to waging war. Leaders of al-Qaeda, Taliban, ISIS, and Boko Haram have quoted 9:5, 9:29, and 9:111.

Most Muslims don't know these verses because most Muslims are non-Arab and don't understand the Arabic of the Qur'an. The Arabic-speaking population is 430 million out of 1.8 billion Muslims.

Many of them may be shocked to learn that the Qur'an allows for Christians and Jews to be attacked and forced to pay the *jizya* (a religious tax forced on non-Muslims). The Muslim fighters of ISIS used this scripture to justify the battle of Mosul of 2016–2017, though later ISIS was defeated. Many Christians lost their lives and belongings because of the jihad declared on their city.

Today in many schools in the Muslim world, jihad is taught as a pillar of Islam in classes to students as young as seven years old, based on verses such as the following:

> Allah has indeed purchased from the believers their lives and wealth in exchange for Paradise. They fight in the cause of Allah and kill or are killed. This is a true promise binding on Him in the Torah, the Gospel, and the Quran. And whose promise is truer than Allah's? So rejoice in the exchange you have made with Him. That is truly the ultimate triumph. (Qur'an 9:111)

Unfortunately, Muslim teaching, in both the Hadith and the Qur'an, holds that Islam is superior to other religions and cultures and that inferior cultures and peoples may be eradicated. What a dark and tragic worldview. Muslims who begin studying their religion closely, such as my late friend Nabeel Qureshi, author of *Seeking Allah, Finding Jesus*, quickly find themselves at an intersection. They must decide whether to become jihadists or to remain cultural Muslims. As long as Muslims read and act on the verses such as the ones mentioned, Islamic terrorism will continue.

Many Muslim women today remain illiterate.[2] Saudi Arabian women were first allowed to drive only in 2018. Child brides are taken in marriage daily across the Muslim world. Children are forbidden to go to school in certain areas. Women are beheaded, stoned, and abused for a variety of infractions. The World Health Organization reports that two hundred million girls and women have undergone female genital mutilation (circumcision) in Muslim countries and that around four million girls are at risk from the grisly ritual every year.[3] Most are mutilated in this way before they reach the age of fifteen.

Churches are burned in Muslim-majority countries such as Iran, Turkey, and Egypt—sometimes frequently. Christian minorities in these and other nations face an uneven legal playing field and encounter restrictions unknown among their Muslim neighbors.

SEEKING SALVATION IN THE DARK

Muslims are generally taught that Christians are immoral worshipers of three gods (not the majestic triune God of Scripture). They are told that Christians have corrupted the Bible. Most of these Muslims have no access to the Bible, of course (such access having been denied to them), and instead must look to the teachings of Islam as their only hope for salvation.[4]

According to Islam, one must pray enough, fast enough, and accomplish the pilgrimage to be saved. It's not surprising, therefore, that many Muslims today aren't sure of their eternal destination. Allah is sovereign and can change his mind on Judgment Day. The Islamic teaching of the "torture of the grave," where Allah sends two angels to interrogate the souls of all who die, added to a works-based system, creates fear and uncertainty in many Muslims.

I was riding a train in North Africa when a man asked me, "Do you speak Arabic?"

I told him I did. He then asked, "Where do you live?"

"In the United States of America."

He said, "America is a bad country."

"You've been there?"

"No, but Americans are illiterate, uneducated, and a bunch of cow herders."

I felt he must mean cowboys. So I asked him, "If you've never been to America, how do you get your information?"

"From television, from movies."

"Sir, there are more than twelve hundred mosques in America." (Today there are over 2,100 mosques in the US.)

He was shocked. "Christianity is outlawed in my country," he said. "You can be imprisoned for being a Christian from a Muslim background."

Muslims today continue to be unaware of how free people are in other countries. This is ironic, since their own countries are largely unfree when it comes to economics, politics, or religion. Many are told that the West is Christian and is therefore immoral. Islamic leaders argue that Islam is a peaceful religion, but no Muslim is allowed to question the life of Muhammad or the teachings of sharia, Islamic religious law.

Jesus's words from Matthew 5:14, "You are the light of the world," draw a contrast with the spiritual darkness of the Muslim world, which leaves millions of God's image-bearers without the opportunity (humanly speaking) of turning to Jesus. Unfortunately, sometimes we believers misinterpret this darkness and what it means. We may even blame Muslims for the darkness. A church elder once confided to me, "I don't believe Muslims deserve the gospel." What a travesty! *No one* deserves the gospel—not even you or me! The spiritual darkness enveloping much of the Muslim world is not an excuse for us to refuse to share the treasure we have in Christ. It should be a holy spur to action!

55 Seconds for Change

We Christians need to move beyond any understandable but misplaced anger about the inequities in the Muslim world to a love for Muslims that can only come from God himself. *Muslims are not our enemies.* Yes, they are blinded to the gospel—as we once were before the Holy Spirit opened our hearts. In compassion we are to shine God's light into the darkness. In studying the history of missions to Muslims, we see that too often the church has avoided rather than engaged the Muslim world. For 1,400 years, millions upon millions of Muslim people have been born, been raised, married, had children, and died—all without ever seeing a page of the New Testament.

Brothers and sisters, this has to change. If you agree, please pray with me:

> *Lord, Muslims are trapped in spiritual darkness. This darkness can't be overcome by argument or anger, but only by your Spirit and prayer. Please lift the veil that covers their eyes. We ask you to defeat the work of the god of this world, who works to blind the minds of unbelievers, including those in Islam. Break down the strongholds, human or demonic, that keep them in spiritual bondage. Give them the hunger that only you can satisfy. Make me faithful in prayer for and in witness to my Muslim neighbors, leaving the results in your all-powerful hands. Amen.*

Chapter 5

OBEDIENCE, GROWTH, AND JOY

During a training program, a new believer approached me. Ali had been a Sunni Muslim who heard the gospel from a believer with a Shia background. After reading the Bible, Ali decided to follow Jesus. That day, Ali asked me to baptize him. We did it in a beautiful lake in Minnesota, and believers from many different cultures, including Sunni and Shia backgrounds, attended his baptism. Only the Messiah Jesus can bring his lost sheep from every corner to be one flock following one Shepherd. What a joyful privilege it was to be one link in the Lord's chain of salvation for Ali.

GROWTH IN OBEDIENCE

Serving among Muslims is a step of obedience. And when we obey, there is joy. When we obey, there is blessing. As with the wonderful feeling I experienced with baptizing a new believer in Minnesota, whenever we serve among Muslims, we experience such joy.

If we are to grow as disciples of Christ, we must evangelize "as we go." But this is no grim duty we are to perform with clenched teeth. Proclaiming Christ enriches us socially, personally, and spiritually. It's one of God's greatest tools for sharpening us.

Ministering to Muslims increases our need to study the Bible. I was a young believer when I began sharing the gospel with my Muslim classmates. It was challenging and frustrating much of the time. The conversations went in many directions, resulting in no real focus.

But my knowledge of the Bible grew as I sought answers to questions I heard from Muslims about God and his character. In 1993 I started Crescent Project to equip other believers to share the gospel with Muslims too. God has now raised up thousands of people who are equipped and reaching Muslims.

One of my greatest joys is listening to testimonies of spiritual growth from our alumni. Many share how ministering to Muslims has increased their faith in the God who loves all people. Others share how their faith has increased by seeing God's sovereignty in opening doors. Others see the power of God to save those we think are too far away to be reached by grace. Others simply have increased their knowledge of the Bible in relation to Islam.

All these experiences share a common thread—a growing and joyful dependency on the grace of God.

GROWTH IN SERVING

When you serve with Muslims, you encounter different cultures and nationalities. I'm excited when I have the opportunity to visit different families and countries. I learn so much from listening to their ideas, their worldviews, and their stories. This doesn't mean I have to agree with their ideas or perceptions—far from it! I know that the Bible is a timeless standard against which we must examine all ideas.

Yet my interactions with different peoples and cultures have increased my awareness of God's beautiful creation. Let's remember that God created diversity; the devil uses it only for division. God is creative and the devil is destructive. Having different groups was God's idea in the first place.

Morocco's culture, for example, is eclectic and has an ancient history. The first time I visited this former French colony in North Africa, several Moroccans invited me to their homes, where we had many deep spiritual conversations. These friends were eager to hear about a God who loves them and seeks a relationship with them that goes far beyond rituals of fasting and washing.

In another country, one of our short-term teams served Syrian Muslim refugees who had arrived on rafts from Turkey. The team helped meet their basic needs while they recovered from the ordeal. They listened as the refugees shared their agonizing stories. Team members were given the opportunity to pray for families who had seen the horrors of the Syrian civil war.

In their obedience, the team members experienced the blessing of obeying our Savior, who says it's better to give than to receive (Acts 20:35). Experiencing this for ourselves deepens our faith in God's grace to us, his goodness, and his wonderful plan for our lives.

The Bible promises, "A generous person will prosper; whoever refreshes others will be refreshed" (Prov. 11:25). I and many other obedient disciples have experienced the lovely truth of this verse.

GROWTH IN MIRACLES OF GRACE

God is actively at work building his church. Sometimes he does this through what I call miracles of grace, when he intervenes in the lives of new believers in dramatic ways. I see those miracles daily—God answering prayers and orchestrating things for the spread of his kingdom. Miracles of grace help us grow. Just a few examples of such miracles I've witnessed include the following:

- An American convert to Islam heard the gospel and received Jesus as Savior and Lord. Jesus the Messiah instantly changed this new believer, removing his previous anxiety and fear.
- An Iraqi refugee heard the gospel and prayed for his family's salvation. Nine months later, he baptized his wife.
- A sixteen-year-old Iraqi immigrant heard the gospel from a friend in the neighborhood. She became a believer and began to pray for her family. In the next twenty months, her sister was saved, and they began praying together for their parents. Her father received Jesus next, and now they are all praying for the mother.
- A Muslim student became a believer in a neighborhood Bible study. When his family found out about his new faith, they persecuted him. Every day they heaped verbal abuse—and sometimes physical abuse—on him. So this small Bible study group asked God to intervene. Soon the student's family stopped the physical abuse, and his home environment began to change. While the parents aren't yet Christians, they are open to discussing spiritual things.

- An Afghan Christian at our annual conference shared her desire for her family members to be saved and asked us to pray that they might move from persecution to salvation. We prayed, asking God to move in special and mighty ways. The next year, she attended the conference with two members of her family. God had answered quickly, beyond our expectations!

As we minister to Muslims, we can expect to see miracles of grace all around us. They empower our witness and edify our souls for a closer walk with the Savior. In the past twenty years, as David Garrison has reported, more Muslims have come to Christ than in the previous 1,400 years.[5] God is actively moving on this planet. Miracles aren't the only way the Lord chooses to work among Muslims, but we should never be surprised that he is moving among them. After all, every Muslim who turns to Jesus Christ is a miracle of God's grace—and what a privilege it is to participate as his messengers.

55 Seconds for Change

Yes, being Christ's ambassador to the Muslim world is a huge responsibility, but one that brings even more joyful benefits in Christian growth when we accept it. May God give us the grace to enjoy deeper fellowship with him and with one another as we walk in obedience.

If that is your desire, please take a moment to pray the following:

Oh, God, often I shrink from your commands out of a misplaced desire to preserve my independence and my time, thinking obedience to you is soul-shrinking drudgery. The truth is, obedience is a sign of love for you, one that opens the door to your blessings. As 1 John 5:3 (ESV) says, "This is the love of God, that we keep his commandments. And his commandments are not burdensome." Sharing the gospel with Muslims brings great blessings to them and to me. I want to progress in my faith! Help me to obey! May I learn to love you more, for your glory and their good. In Jesus's name. Amen.

Chapter 6

YOUR SPIRITUAL WALK

A small group of Christians at a church in California began a new study called "Bridges: Christians Connecting with Muslims." Some of the attendees complained, wondering why they needed to study Islam and share the gospel with Muslims. Yet as the evening progressed, these members found themselves repenting of their previously unrecognized hatred of Muslims. One even committed to inviting his Muslim neighbor to a Thanksgiving meal at his home.

God can melt the hard hearts of his people when it comes to reaching out to Muslims with the good news—and he does this all the time! In the last twenty-five years, Crescent Project has seen thousands come alongside our efforts to share Christ with Muslims.

Yes, there is no doubt that training is important, and we try to provide excellent training to help Christians share effectively. But there is no substitute for a strong walk with Jesus. The more you know the Savior, the more you shine. Knowing Jesus is to have a daily walk with him. He is our strength and sufficiency as we share the gospel with Muslims. That's what we will look at in this chapter.

In recent years, many ministries to Muslims have begun to argue about what constitutes the most effective "tools" for reaching Muslims. Frankly, I'm sometimes shocked at the level of intensity we show in arguing about methods. This focus on tools and methods, while certainly necessary in Muslim ministry, is not sufficient. These arguments take away from our burden and goal to love our Muslim neighbors.

Jesus's priority was that all people hear the gospel (Mark 16:15; Matt. 28:18–20). His strategy was to teach and call the disciples (2 Tim. 2:2). His method is the best method, and his method is *us*. We are chosen by Jesus to reach Muslims. We are the hands and feet of the Savior. We are the best method of outreach: people reaching people. Each one reach one! While this book will gladly highlight some of the practical ways we can share the gospel, the *sine qua non* of evangelism is our walk with Christ.

WE ARE THE MESSAGE

Ministry flows out of our walk with Jesus. If you aren't close to the Savior, you won't be motivated to talk about him. Your inner conviction, your commitment in word and deed to follow the Messiah Jesus, is the solid foundation for any witnessing you do. The great evangelist and preacher George Whitefield (1714–1770) once said, "We can preach the gospel of Christ no further than we have experienced the power of it in our own hearts."[6]

With that insight in mind, here are some basic spiritual principles that we must master as a foundation for our witness.

Our Identity in Christ

It's imperative that we see ourselves as God sees us. We spend too much time listening to what others say about us instead of what God says about us.

When I received Jesus as my Savior, I also received some specific spiritual benefits. Our salvation is a gift of grace from God that we receive by faith. I act on my faith by trusting Jesus. I trust in his atoning death. I trust in his resurrection. I trust that God forgave me. I trust that Christ lives in me. And I also trust that what the Bible says of me and you is true. The Bible says:

- *You were created:* "Before I formed you in the womb I knew you, before you were born I set you apart; I appointed you as a prophet to the nations" (Jer. 1:5).
- *You were redeemed:* "You know that it was not with perishable things such as silver or gold that you were redeemed from the empty way of life handed down to you from your ancestors" (1 Peter 1:18).
- *You were seated:* "God raised us up with Christ and seated us with him in the heavenly realms in Christ Jesus" (Eph. 2:6).

Are any of these statements about your identity in Christ new to you? The Bible is full of promises and descriptions of our new life in Christ. We are those who bear his name. We carry his identity, and so we want to honor him. One vital way we do this is through our willing obedience—including the obedience of evangelism.

Assurance of Salvation

In Revelation 3:20, Jesus Christ says, "Here I am! I stand at the door and knock. If anyone hears my voice and opens the door, I will come in and eat with that person, and they with me." In this verse Christ is asking to be your leader, special guest, and friend. When Christ enters your life, you become a new creation. Jesus does not lie—when you ask him to enter, he *will* enter. You don't need to keep inviting him.

What a joy to know that we belong to Jesus and to no one else. This assurance gives us hope for the future. This assurance, so different from the uncertainty Islam and other religious traditions offer, gives us confidence when facing Judgment Day and eternity.

You are reading this book, but is your name written in the Book of Life? Have you asked Jesus to be your Savior and Lord? If you have, then he has entered your life as he promised, and you are now a part of his family. If you aren't sure, then why not make a clean break of your sins right now, ask for his forgiveness, and begin the joyous journey with your Savior? Following is not always easy, but he is worth it. Nothing in this life can ever separate you from Christ's love and grace (Rom. 8:31–39). He will take care of you.

The Spirit-Filled Life

In 1 Corinthians 2:14–3:6, we read about three types of people: natural, spiritual, and worldly. The natural person, of course, does not know the Savior. The worldly person is a Christian but one who never takes a stand; he is neither hot nor cold, living on personal energy and power rather than on the Spirit of the living God. The spiritual person, by contrast, walks in the power of the Spirit day by day. What does that look like?

God wants us to be in constant fellowship with him. We are designed that way and work best when we constantly draw from the Lord's living water. Many of us, however, foolishly try to slake our spiritual thirst with such things as friends, career, habits, and hobbies. But only a Spirit-filled and Spirit-guided life will fulfill our hearts and empower us for service.

In John 14, Jesus said he would send an advocate who would live in us and give us power to glorify his name. This is the Holy Spirit, the Spirit of Almighty God. That same Holy Spirit fills us, and by him we are renewed in our character and actions.

HOW TO BE FILLED WITH THE SPIRIT

When you received Jesus, you were indwelled by the spirit of God. But that is only the beginning. The Bible commands those who believe in him to *be filled* with the Spirit. The command is to be obeyed. The following biblical insights revolutionized my walk with Christ as I learned to be filled with the Spirit.

Consecrate Your Life

> *I urge you, brothers and sisters, in view of God's mercy, to offer your bodies as a living sacrifice, holy and pleasing to God—this is your true and proper worship. Do not conform to the pattern of this world, but be transformed by the renewing of your mind. Then you will be able to test and approve what God's will is—his good, pleasing and perfect will.*
> —ROMANS 12:1–2

As this passage shows, we are to lay everything on the line for God—our bodies and our minds. We do this not to empty ourselves of mental or physical health but to fill ourselves with the cleansing and empowering presence of the Spirit. What area of your life is most difficult to surrender to Christ? Don't hesitate. Commit your talents, gifts, abilities, and time—give it all to him. Say, "Lord, I surrender it to you." Just as a sacrifice is offered and belongs on the altar, likewise your life belongs to Jesus.

Confess Your Sins

If we confess our sins, he is faithful and just and will forgive us our sins and purify us from all unrighteousness.
—1 JOHN 1:9

When God convicts you of sin, confess; don't argue or attempt to justify it with God. Ask God to fill you with the Holy Spirit's power. Jesus says we will receive power—including the power to live a godly life—when the Holy Spirit comes. The Christian walk is impossible without the power of the Holy Spirit.

Ask God to Fill You

Do not get drunk on wine, which leads to debauchery. Instead, be filled with the Spirit.
—EPHESIANS 5:18

Ask God to fill you with his Holy Spirit, who is our Guide. If we're not in tune with him, our words will be like clanging cymbals—meaningless to those who need to hear the good news. Each day, and each encounter with a non-Christian, must be given to the Holy Spirit.

Cultivate the Fruit of the Spirit

The fruit of the Spirit is love, joy, peace, patience, kindness, goodness, faithfulness, gentleness and self-control.
—GALATIANS 5:22–23 NIV 1984

No one can give you these character qualities except the Spirit of Christ. You can't purchase them or bribe God with religious rituals to obtain them. These are gifts, and they authenticate the wonderful message of Jesus that we are privileged to share.

55 Seconds for Change

Take a minute and dwell on the fruit of the Spirit. Jot down what these words mean in your life. How would they show up in your ministry to Muslims? Or, for that matter, in ministering to anyone?

Love: _____

Joy: _____

Peace: _____

Patience: _____

Kindness: _____

Goodness: _____

Faithfulness: _____

Gentleness: _____

Self-control: _____

I hope you enjoyed this quick exercise. May you see yourself as God sees you, because you belong to him. Jesus says in John 15:15-16, "I no longer call you servants, because a servant does not know his master's business. Instead, I have called you friends, for everything that I learned from my Father I have made known to you. You did not choose me, but I chose you and appointed you so that you might go and bear fruit—fruit that will last—and so that whatever you ask in my name the Father will give you."

Part 2

HOW TO
BEGIN

Chapter 7

ADOPTING BIBLICAL ATTITUDES

O n a flight from Vienna to Paris, I had the window seat next to a young man who looked Lebanese. He began a conversation with me in English, asking whether I lived in Austria or France. My flight was after ten days of ministry in Europe, driving and speaking in three countries. I was physically and mentally tired, and I wasn't eager to talk right then. I needed sleep; I wasn't the Energizer Bunny.

But this nice young man continued to speak about the beauty of Vienna, how it's the most economical city in Europe. Then he asked me what I did.

"I'm a minister of the gospel," I said. "I teach on similarities between Islam and Christianity."

He pulled out his Arabic Qur'an and told me his name was Omar. Omar and I chuckled that we were speaking in English, not knowing we were both from Lebanon.

Omar defended Islam, claiming it is the most peaceful religion. I prayed silently for my attitude to change as I moved the conversation to the uniqueness of the Bible. By the time we

49

had landed in Paris, Omar had committed to downloading a Bible app and considering the teachings of Jesus.

During my flight to Paris, I needed a change of attitude. It's true I was tired, but God has a plan for my life. *All* appointments are divine appointments. My role is to reflect Christ in my life. As Proverbs 4:23 says, "Above all else, guard your heart, for everything you do flows from it."

Our attitudes inevitably impact our behavior toward and communication with Muslims. What are the basic attitudes we need to effectively witness about Jesus?

TAKE THE INITIATIVE

In Matthew 28:18–20, Jesus is asking us to take the initiative. Let us always be ready to share. Nabeel Qureshi, in his book *Seeking Allah, Finding Jesus*, asked why it took so long for people to talk to him about Jesus. This question is echoed by many other Muslim-background believers in Christ. Some were born in Western countries but didn't hear the gospel until they were in their late twenties.

While walking on the streets of Madrid, Spain, serving on a ministry trip, I saw an Arab man with his son, who was riding a tricycle in front of their apartment. I greeted them. I told the man I was from Beirut, visiting Madrid for the first time. Khalid was from Morocco. We discussed some of the similarities among the Mediterranean cultures of Spain, Morocco, and Lebanon. It was during Ramadan, so Khalid asked me, "Are you fasting?"

"I am fasting the Jesus way," I said. "Since I decided to follow Jesus."

"What is fasting the Jesus way?"

"I can't tell you," I said with a smile, "since Jesus says that when you fast, no one should know except God."

Khalid chuckled and said that the news media always cover when Muslims fast. I asked him if he had read the Injeel. He hadn't but asked for one. We gladly gave him an Arabic copy.

We weren't shy and took the initiative, allowing God to guide the conversation. There is no need to avoid the subject of Jesus, deciding that others are not interested. Many Muslims *are* eager to hear about our faith.

REPRESENT CHRIST

Second Corinthians 5:20 calls us "Christ's ambassadors." Ambassadors represent a country, but making people citizens of that country is not part of their job description. My role is simply to share, not to convert; God does the converting. He works in the hearts of Muslims, and I'm just his representative.

In witness to Muslims there is often a tension between appealing to reason and appealing to revelation. Should I reason with a Muslim friend for the truth of the gospel, or simply expect God to reveal himself to him or her? Either way, I'm just an ambassador, pointing people to the Messiah Jesus. Whether they accept the message or not, whether they agree with me or not, I have one objective—to share the words of Jesus.

TELL THE TRUTH

One January, while visiting Texas, I decided to meet with one of my best friends in downtown Austin. After I parked and started walking, I noticed throngs of women converging on the downtown. It turned out that thirty-four thousand women were rallying in support of women rights, fair treatment, and an end to abuse.

It was awesome to see people stand up for truth, but I was deeply disappointed that their message of equality and safety wasn't complete. You see, there were no signs against stoning women in the Muslim world. No signs against beheadings in the name of sharia law. I didn't see any signs demanding that Muslim women be educated. While it had noble goals, the rally failed to discuss the *whole* truth about women's issues in the twenty-first century, particularly in Muslim-majority countries.

Friends, in sharing the love of God with Muslims, we must be committed to sharing the truth of God and to doing so in love. Many times we avoid speaking the truth so we won't offend. We must not shy away, for Jesus promises, "You will know the truth, and the truth will set you free" (John 8:32).

Today, few people discuss the suffering of women in the Muslim world. Few address life issues that have enslaved and demeaned them for years. As we share with our Muslim friends, let us be committed to sharing the truth of the Bible in regard to all subjects. As we share that truth, gently but forthrightly, we can expect the Holy Spirit to convict hearts and soften them to the good news of forgiveness and grace in Christ.

HAVE COMPASSION

In John 3:16 we see the love of God. The God of the Bible demonstrates his love daily. Today more than ever, Muslims need to see *our* love in action. Many of them are suffering, and all of them need God's love. They don't need more religion or fanaticism; they need the love of the Christian community.

All people are invited to join the family of Christ. The Messiah commanded us to go to all to share his love and his message. Our teams serving among refugees in Europe and the Middle East see Muslims regularly respond to their compassion. *Your* Muslim friend might have suffered a trauma from civil war, sectarian violence, or social oppression. Respect your Muslim friends by listening to and empathizing with their journey. God's love melts the hardest of hearts. Jesus's love always wins!

USE THE POWER TO PROCLAIM

The events of September 11, 2001, have scarred our society with a lasting fear of Muslims. This is understandable, as much of the Islamic world continues to experience strife and jihad. Yet we need to separate the religion from the people.

Many Christians turn angry and hateful whenever they learn of terrorist attacks. Yes, committed Christians *should* be angry that innocent lives are wasted for political and religious gain. I hope we are angry when we see stabbings and shootings. But Jesus asks us to be angry and still not sin (Eph. 4:26). May God remove this hatefulness and replace it with compassion and conviction.

The majority of Muslims are not militant. Most are rather decent people who seek to know the will of God for their lives—just like we do. Sadly, however, many times we share the good news in a combative and angry manner, as if we are on a battlefield. The truth is, many Muslims are eager to hear about Jesus, and our ministry sees many of them get baptized and follow him. Even those who have not made a commitment are reading the Bible.

An Iranian doctor walked into a church one Monday morning and asked if anyone was willing to tell him about becoming a Christian. The pastor met with him. The doctor indicated he had been reading the Bible for the last ten years on his own, and he was convinced that Jesus is the Savior.

This man was soon baptized as a believer in Christ.

While not all the spiritual fruit we will encounter among Muslims will be this ripe, we can speak confidently, for Jesus said in the Great Commission, "I am with you always, to the very end of the age" (Matt. 28:20). This promise gives us courage to proclaim the good news. Courage isn't the absence of fear, but rather action in spite of fear. Our courage comes from the Savior.

Remember that thirty seconds of courage on your part can change the life of a Muslim for eternity.

BUILD BRIDGES

When conversing with Muslims, maintain an attitude of listening and learning. Build bridges. There are many points of tension between Islam and Christianity. So start with the many similarities.[7]

Of course, we must always move beyond common ground and *cross the bridge*. The goal of a bridge is to cross. Sometimes we get stuck discussing commonalities with Islam and we're afraid to move to the message of salvation, which is that God loves all people and he sent Jesus to be the Savior. We will cover more about building bridges in the next chapter.

OFFER BIBLICAL ANSWERS

We often try to answer questions posed by Muslims using logic, reason, and history. These are all right as far as they go, but the key foundation for any answer should be the Bible. It's the guide for our understanding of life and our relationship with God. Sharing biblical answers will confirm to our Muslim friends that we are true believers in Christ. If the Bible is our foundation, they will consider reading it, even if only out of curiosity. Our goal is to help Muslims see the beauty and power of the Bible.

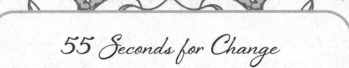

55 Seconds for Change

Here are a couple of hints to help you communicate God's truth winsomely:

- Find Bible passages that answer your friend's questions. Numerous passages deal with life issues. If your friend reads these passages, he or she will want to read more. The Bible is reasonable in its words and message. Consequently, God is revealed through the text.
- Always offer your Muslim friend a Bible, or portions of it, such as the book of John or the book of Luke. Let the Holy Spirit use the words of Scripture to draw your friend to faith. Depend on the powerful promise we find in Isaiah:

> As the rain and the snow
> come down from heaven,
> and do not return to it
> without watering the earth
> and making it bud and flourish,
> so that it yields seed for the sower and bread for
> the eater,
> so is my word that goes out from my mouth:
> It will not return to me empty,
> but will accomplish what I desire
> and achieve the purpose for which I sent it."
> (Isa. 55:10-11)

Chapter 8

OVERCOMING FEAR

When I was a teenager, the nighttime fighting around our home in Beirut was scary. I had no idea what the future held—or even if I would have a future. During these times, my father would open his Bible and read, in Arabic, Psalm 91:

> Whoever dwells in the shelter of the Most High
>> will rest in the shadow of the Almighty.
> I will say of the Lord, "He is my refuge and my fortress,
>> my God, in whom I trust."

> Surely he will save you
>> from the fowler's snare
>> and from the deadly pestilence.
> He will cover you with his feathers,
>> and under his wings you will find refuge;
>> his faithfulness will be your shield and rampart.
> You will not fear the terror of night,
>> nor the arrow that flies by day,
> nor the pestilence that stalks in the darkness,
>> nor the plague that destroys at midday.

A thousand may fall at your side,
>   ten thousand at your right hand,
>   but it will not come near you.
You will only observe with your eyes
>   and see the punishment of the wicked.

If you say, "The LORD is my refuge,"
>   and you make the Most High your dwelling,
no harm will overtake you,
>   no disaster will come near your tent.
For he will command his angels concerning you
>   to guard you in all your ways;
they will lift you up in their hands,
>   so that you will not strike your foot against
>   a stone.
You will tread on the lion and the cobra;
>   you will trample the great lion and the serpent.

"Because he loves me," says the LORD, "I will
>   rescue him;
I will protect him, for he acknowledges my name.
He will call on me, and I will answer him;
>   I will be with him in trouble,
>   I will deliver him and honor him.
With long life I will satisfy him
>   and show him my salvation."

These amazing promises of God's protection sustained me during the long nights of uncertainty and laid a solid foundation for my life and ministry today. They took away my fear and enabled me to trust the Lord.

HEALTHY AND UNHEALTHY FEAR

Fear is an emotion we all experience. It helps to protect us from situations and actions that might cause physical or emotional harm, and in that sense, it is a good thing. But that is not the only kind of fear. Some fear keeps us from doing the right thing, such as sharing our faith.

Once I was speaking to a Syrian Sunni Muslim who acted condescendingly toward me. When he belittled a well-known Christian apologist, Nabeel Qureshi, I knew my attitude was heading in the wrong direction and that my anger and fear were not from my Savior. I had to adjust my attitude, and fast!

Let's face it, friend. The prospect of witnessing tends to create at least some level of fear in most of us. If the person with whom you hope to share the good news is a Muslim, you can expect your fear quotient to ratchet still higher. But if you're going to take the next step and present the gospel, that fear must be overcome.

The Bible speaks to the kind of unhealthy fear that comes from acting in our own strength, without depending on God. This soul-crippling fear keeps us from obeying Christ's commands. Yet this fear and anxiety can be overcome if the Word of God is our foundation.

Jesus says, "Peace I leave with you; my peace I give you. I do not give to you as the world gives. Do not let your hearts be troubled and do not be afraid" (John 14:27). This promise applies to every believer. Peace is his gift to us, so why do we experience fear and anxiety when we want to share our faith? Maybe because we fail to appropriate it.

As Ephesians 6:10–18 reminds us, we must put on our

spiritual armor. The battle for souls goes far deeper than politics, education, or religious differences. The battle is for the hearts and minds of human beings everywhere. The enemy is like a roaring lion (1 Peter 5:8), and his goal is to disrupt what God is doing in your life and ultimately to destroy you. In the famous book *Pilgrim's Progress*, Christian sees a roaring lion that frightens everyone. But then, to his great relief, Christian sees that the lion is chained.

So it is with our Christian lives. The Messiah has already crushed the serpent (Gen. 3:15) by his death and resurrection. The devil is bound (Mark 3:26–28), and we get to plunder his house in the name of Jesus. Speak to your Muslim friends and coworkers by faith (2 Cor. 4:13), for the Lord is building his church, and the gates of hell will not prevail against it (Matt. 16:17–19).

Now, it is true that the devil has blinded people through false religion, materialism, and selfishness (2 Cor. 4:4), but he does not get the final word. The Son of God appeared to "destroy the devil's work" (1 John 3:8).

We are part of his plan to destroy those works. Therefore, when I experience fear, I need to realize that it isn't from my conquering Savior. It's instead an arrow from the conquered Evil One, who puts fear into our hearts to distract us from obeying the Great Commission. Thank God that we can defeat this arrow with the shield of faith (Eph. 6:16), faith that Jesus is the Lord not only of the universe but also of that moment of fear. Jesus has all the authority (Matt. 28:18), and this is his time for me to share the gospel (2 Cor. 6:2).

Whether on a mission trip, in a ministry setting, or in a friend's living room, remember the following points. They will help you conquer fear. Jesus is with you.

How to Engage in Spiritual Warfare

1. ***Relinquish control to God.*** You must, by an act of will, decide that God is the one who steers your life (Matt. 16:24–26; Prov. 16:3). His will is the goal you are to strive for at all times (Matt. 6:10).

2. ***Pray for discernment.*** There will be times when you're not sure exactly what to do, even if you're obedient to God's will. Ask him to provide the wisdom you need (James 1:5), through his Holy Spirit (John 16:13), to discern the path you should take (Ps. 37:23).

3. ***Depend on the Holy Spirit.*** Acts 1:8 is clear that the Holy Spirit's power is seen in our being witnesses for Jesus. It is the spirit of God that gives us the strength and the courage to share what Christ has done in our life. Whenever you talk about the Messiah Jesus, remember that the spirit of God is present and convicts people of the righteousness of God.

4. ***Do nothing from your own strength.*** Your strength isn't adequate to the task of witnessing, so stop acting as if it is. Depend on his power (Zech. 4:6). In John 15 Christ gives a practical picture of our daily walk with him, comparing our relationship to him to the one between the vine and the branches. The branch can't bear fruit of its own; it must abide in the vine. Likewise, our strength for the task comes directly from Christ. Your daily study of the Word and daily prayer help you abide in Christ. Trust him to lead and give you the right words and attitudes to build a bridge with your Muslim friend.

5. ***Act with courage.*** Don't be passive when experiencing fear and anxiety. Pray over your home, your family, your work, and your relationships! In prayer, build a wall of protection around you and your family and your friendships (Ps. 91). Prayer changes things! God will empower you to be a bold, courageous witness for Christ (Acts 1:8).

55 Seconds for Change

As you think about the fear and anxiety you must confront in your life, I invite you to read the following verses. Then, over the next ten days, meditate over one verse each morning or evening when you have your quiet time with the Lord. Let God's Word, not your fear, rule your mind. The words *do not be afraid* are mentioned 365 times in the Bible. God affirms you daily with the promise of his presence with you.

Psalm 56:3

Philippians 4:4–8

Joshua 1:9

John 14:27

2 Thessalonians 3:16

Psalm 4:8

Isaiah 26:3–4

Jeremiah 17:7–8

Romans 8:38–39

Hebrews 13:5–6

Chapter 9

STARTING A
CONVERSATION

Recently I was sitting beside a medical doctor on an airplane. From his accent and appearance, I suspected he was from the Middle East. I also knew it was near the end of Ramadan, the month of ritual fasting for Muslims. So I opened the conversation with a simple greeting: "Ramadan Mubarak," which means, "God bless you in this month of Ramadan."

This blessing opened the door to further conversation. My new Muslim friend, who was living in Atlanta, and I spoke of our common origin in the Middle East. By the time the plane landed, we'd spoken at length about Islam and Christianity, particularly about the question of whether God's Word can be changed. He accepted a copy of my book *Is the Injeel Corrupted?*

How should we broach the subject of Christ when we meet a Muslim? I think it's helpful to use words that connect with Muslim hearts and minds. The beginning of the conversation is just as important as how it ends—maybe even more. In this chapter let's sharpen our skills in starting and leading healthy conversations about our Savior. Let's start with a look at some basic Muslim beliefs and rituals and end with practical ways to begin talking with a Muslim friend.

FIVE BASIC ISLAMIC BELIEFS

When you open a conversation with Muslims, it's helpful to know something about their *faith* or *belief.* In the context of their religion, how do Muslims think?

1. One God

The first and most important Islamic belief is the worship of one God. Qur'an 2:255–258 describes the worship of Allah. Allah is the name of God in Arabic.[8]

How do you come to know God in Islam? Muslims will tell you, "Know God through his beautiful names." So they like to teach one another what are called the ninety-nine beautiful names of God. In reality, the Qur'an mentions 104 names for Allah, but ninety-nine is a magical number in Islam. *Allahu al-Barry* means "God the creator." *Allahu al-Qudoos* means "God is holy." *Allahu al-Raheem* means "God is merciful." *Allahu al-Malek* means "God the sovereign king."

We Christians like a lot of these names because they agree with what the Bible teaches about God and his character. But some of the names disagree with what the Bible says. One, *Allahu al-Mumeet,* means "God is the source of death." Christians believe that God is the giver of life and that death entered the world because of sin (see Rom. 5:12–21).

Another, *Allahu al-Muntaqim,* means "the avenger." When you study the verse that uses this name in the Qur'an, you encounter the concept of God coming after you in vengeance, rather than justice.

A third troubling name for Allah is *Allahu al-Macker*. Qur'an 3:54 and 8:30 say not to scheme against God because God is the best schemer. This is the exact meaning of the qur'anic verse as it references the scheming nature of Allah. The idea is that he may follow his whim rather than his promise. So when you ask a good Muslim, "Are you going to heaven?" he may reply, "I hope so, if God wills." In Islam, you can be the best Muslim and still miss out on heaven because God can change his mind.

The implication of a couple of these names is that God can't be trusted. He can be both evil and good at the same time. Most Muslims worry about their eternal destiny and use the rituals of Islam to protect themselves, they hope, from God's wrath. The Bible, by contrast, portrays God as a heavenly Father (Matt. 6:32), as the giver of good things (Matt. 7:11), the giver of life (Ps. 36:9), the maker and keeper of promises (2 Cor. 1:20–22), and the One who brings good even out of evil (Gen. 50:20; Rom. 8:28).

Muslims believe that the Allah of the Qur'an is the true God and that we Christians have changed the teachings of the Bible to come up with a false picture of God. Some Muslims also believe that Christianity and Islam worship different numbers of gods—three for us, one for them. But, in reality, we both worship one God.

What word do we use for God when speaking with Muslims? *God*, of course, is the common word in English. Muslims use the word *Allah*, which might be a contraction of the Arabic *al-ilāh*, "the God." Its root might be *el*, or *eloah*, which is used in the Hebrew Bible as one of the ways to describe God. In some languages, Christians too have used this word for God for centuries.

When I'm talking to a Muslim in Arabic, I use *Allah*. If I'm talking to him in English, I use *God*. If he insists on *Allah*, I say, "Fine. Let's talk about Allah. Who is Allah?" And I lead him to understand the Allah of the Bible.

Several character qualities of Allah in the Qur'an contradict those of God in the Bible. The Qur'an goes so far as to say that God loves only Muslims and no one else. But that contradicts the Bible's teaching that God loves everyone, even though we all sin and fall short of obeying his commandments.

2. *Angels, Demons, and* Jinn

A second basic teaching of Islam is that angels exist, including demons and *jinn*. (Christians, following the witness of Scripture, believe in the first two.) Muslims believe angels are created from light, while demons are created from fire. (Christians believe God created angels as his servants and that demons are fallen angels who chose to ally with the devil, the chief fallen angel.) Islam and Islamic cultures mention some forty types of *jinn*, or genies, which are half-human, half-demon and tend to be regarded as controlled by Satan.

Most Muslims fear the jinn. Many seek power sources and rituals to protect themselves from the misfortunes that the jinn bring. This fear permeates all aspects of Muslim life, including business. Fearful Muslims use amulets and protection verses to bless certain locations and individuals.

3. *God's Prophets*

Third, Muslims believe in God's prophets. Many of the prophets mentioned in the Qur'an are also found in the Bible, which is much older, particularly the Old Testament. The Qur'an doesn't include the stories and details of their lives, but it does mention them by name. Jonah is mentioned, which allows us to utilize his story to lead Muslim friends to Christ (see Matt. 12:38–41).

John the Baptist is mentioned as a prophet, which makes it easy for you to ask your Muslim friend, "If John the Baptist is a prophet, what did he come to do?" The answer—that he came to prepare the way for the Messiah (see John 1:23)—leads the conversation right to Jesus. Even the Qur'an says that Jesus was the Messiah of the Jewish people (Qur'an 4:171; 3:45; 3:49–50; 5:46).

The Qur'an teaches that, among others, Adam, Noah, Moses, Job, Elijah, and Elisha were all prophets. Yet orthodox Islam (followed by the vast majority of Sunni Muslims) teaches that Muhammad is the *seal*—that is, the last—of the prophets.

While Bible-believing Christians disagree about the prophetic status of some individuals whom Islam describes as prophets (for example, the Qur'an says that Alexander the Great was a prophet), let's not emphasize our differences when speaking with Muslims about Jesus. Rather, let's focus on the beliefs we share—such as the truth that God sends prophets to lead people to faith.

4. God's Messages

Islam teaches not only that God sent prophets but also that through them he sent four messages. The person who brings one of God's messages is called a *rasul*, a messenger. So Muhammad and three other prophets bear the title rasul, an exalted category.

What are the four messages that a Muslim must believe and obey? According to the Qur'an, the first is the Tawrat, the Book of Moses; the second is the Zabur, the Psalms of David; the third is the Injeel (literally "the good news"), the Book of Jesus (the New Testament); and the fourth is the Qur'an, the Book of Muhammad. The Qur'an itself says that God sent the fourth message to confirm the previous three, *not* to replace them (Qur'an 3:2–3).

However, Islamic teachers don't seem to agree with that statement, as they don't teach from the Old or New Testaments. Why don't Islamic teachers teach the Tawrat of Moses? Because they believe these messages have been corrupted. Most imams teach that Allah sent the Tawrat of Moses and the Zabur of David but that the Jewish people corrupted these messages. They claim also that although Allah sent the Injeel of Jesus, the Christians changed it. Therefore, Islamic teachers say, Allah sent his fourth and final message, the Qur'an, the book of Muhammad. They claim the Qur'an cannot be corrupted.

5. *Judgment Day*

Islam teaches of a coming Judgment Day, when everybody will be raised from the dead and will stand before God. Imams teach that God is a shrewd businessman—that is, he can't be cheated. Life is a test, and on Judgment Day your good works are put on one side of a scale and your bad works on the other. How the scale tips determines whether you go to heaven or hell. According to Islam, each person has an angel on the right who keeps track of his good works and an angel on the left who keeps track of the bad works.

The Islamic heaven is a sensual paradise with food, drink, and women for the sexual pleasure of men. Hell is a place of eternal fire, where your skin burns off and God creates new skin to burn, over and over again. Most Muslims are terribly afraid of Judgment Day. Allah is sovereign; he can do whatever he wants, and he makes no guarantees to anyone.

RITUALS: WHAT MUST MUSLIMS DO

Now we turn from how Muslims think to focus on how they behave. What are their religious practices? The life of a practicing Muslim is built on the five pillars of Islam. These are five rituals, some of which are performed daily, and one of which is expected only once in a person's lifetime. A practicing Muslim performs these five rituals in a lifelong effort to become pleasing to God, storing up good deeds in hopes that their sins will be erased on Judgment Day.

We study these practices because we want to understand our Muslim friends—the aspects of their lives that are most important to them, that shape their worldview and their deepest drives. Every element of Islamic belief and practice that is similar to Christian belief and practice can serve as a starting point for building bridges from Islam to salvation in Christ.

1. *The Islamic Creed:* Al-Shahadah

The word *shahadah* means "to testify." This is the creed of Islam, which goes: "There is no God except Allah, and Muhammad is his messenger." Reciting this creed in the presence of a Muslim makes you a Muslim. It implies a commitment to follow the example and teachings of Muhammad.

The shahadah is often treated as a magical statement. In a home, you might find it framed in Arab calligraphy and hung on the wall. When a baby is born, the father or grandfather whispers the creed in the baby's ear, making him or her a Muslim. The shahadah is always recited before and after prayer. It's an important part of the Muslim's daily ritual.

2. *Islamic Prayer:* Al-Salat

Salat is the prayer ceremony a Muslim must perform in the mosque or alone five times a day. The word means "to bow down," and it has been borrowed from Christian terminology in Syria. The five prayer times are sunrise, noon, afternoon (two hours after noon), sunset, and then two hours after sunset.

A Muslim must pray facing Mecca, which means, for those of us west of Arabia, facing east, and for those east of Arabia, facing west. Before each prayer, a Muslim must perform ablutions, or ritual washing. Between ablutions and prayer, the Muslim cannot touch a Jew, a Christian, a pagan, or a member of the opposite sex, or he or she would be defiled, and the ablutions would have to be performed all over again.

When it's time to pray, the Muslim stands and recites the first chapter (seven verses) of the Qur'an. Then he or she kneels and bows—knees, palms, and forehead all touching the ground. Each prayer requires a certain number of kneelings—some four, some three, some two. And since tradition says that Muhammad always added an extra kneeling, Muslims usually add an extra kneeling to each prayer. The extra one is meant to be counted by the aforementioned angel on the right.

3. *The Islamic Month of Fasting:* Al-Saum

During *al-Saum*, the lunar month of twenty-eight or twenty-nine days during Ramadan, Muslims aren't allowed to eat during daylight hours, but they compensate for the foregone meals by feasting at night. Islam follows a lunar year that is eleven or twelve days shorter than the Western calendar, so the month of Ramadan rotates gradually through the seasons. The final night of Ramadan is called *Laylat al-Qadar*—the Night of Destiny, or Power. On this night God might answer one's prayers for the upcoming year. Most Muslims like to spend the night chanting the Qur'an or listening to it being chanted. Some read it.

If you know someone who is fasting for Ramadan, pray for him or her on that final night. That's the time of greatest focus on God. God often uses that night to grant dreams or visions or to send someone to talk to a Muslim about Jesus.

4. *Islamic Giving:* Al-Zakat

The word *zakat* comes from a Hebrew root meaning "to purify," implying that giving to the needy purifies the rest of your money and earns you credit for good works.

Sunnis give 2.5 percent of their annual income, while Shiites give 5 percent. Some Muslim cultures today have tried to organize a financial structure for Muslims to pay *zakat*, but in most places *zakat* isn't organized. Nonetheless, even without such a structure, many Muslims help the poor spontaneously, as they see the need.

5. *The Islamic Pilgrimage:* Al-Hajj

Al-hajj, the pilgrimage to Mecca and Medina, is the highest of all the rituals. Every able Muslim is required to make this pilgrimage at least once in his or her lifetime.

Most years, the hajj to Mecca attracts 2 to 3 million pilgrims. When they arrive, men shave their heads and clip their fingernails. Men put on the customary two-piece wool garment, and women wear robes. They enter *Masjid al-Haram*, the largest mosque in the world, and walk around the *Ka'aba*, which houses "the Black Stone," seven times counterclockwise. As they walk, they must touch the stone, which is a meteorite that fell in

Arabia before Islam. The Arabs, who were pagan at the time, thought it was a gift from the god of heaven, so they placed it in the Ka'aba. As many pilgrims as possible try to follow Muhammad's example and kiss the stone. The pilgrimage also involves visiting Medina and other sites, commemorating the events of Muhammad's flight from Mecca in AD 622, marking the beginning of the Muslim calendar.

Once a faithful Muslim returns from the pilgrimage, he or she is called *hajji*, meaning one who has accomplished hajj. One of my friends went on hajj twenty-one times. I asked him why, and he answered, "Every time I went and came back, I had not found peace." His search for inner peace ended only when he found Christ.

55 Seconds for Change

Today there is a resurgence of Islamic ritual. Muslims are reading Islamic books and watching Islamic programs. There is a huge presence of Muslim sites and outreach endeavors on social media, and Islam appears as a pious and growing religion. Rituals are nice but should not be used to control God. Piety is commendable but does not replace a repentant heart. This understanding of Islam compels us to share with Muslims the hope we have in Christ.

There are many common points between Muslim and Christian beliefs and rituals that we can build on to communicate effectively with our Muslim friends. Commit now to see Muslims as people who are thirsty for salvation. Commit to being a part of helping Muslims see the beauty of the teachings of Christ.

Abba Father, thank you that many Muslims are pious and care to worship you. Thank you for preparing hearts to see the need for salvation. Change my heart. Give me your eyes to see Muslims around me in a fresh way. I commit to sharing your hopeful message with all those I meet. Make me an instrument in your hands to share the hope with Muslims. You are worthy. To you belong all glory, power, and majesty. Amen.

Chapter 10

BUILDING
FRIENDSHIPS
WITH MUSLIMS

You don't need a PhD in Islam to build a friendship with a Muslim. The basic information about Muslims' beliefs and practices shared in the previous chapter will serve as a great starting point. Your grasp of his or her basic beliefs and rituals will show respect and understanding.

So how to start? In my thirty-plus years of ministry among Muslims, I have learned to always step out in faith. When we show up in Jesus's name, in Jesus's authority, God moves. Your first step is to take the initiative, to disciple as you go.

An Algerian doctoral student once asked me if I understood American culture. It was an observation of the tendency of Western people to avoid relationships or conversations with Muslims. We've been influenced to avoid these conversations. On the other hand, our Savior and Master commanded us to start these conversations (Matt. 28:18–20). This Algerian man wasn't a theologian or even a practicing Muslim. He was just looking for friendship.

Begin by praying silently for God to open the conversation. My pastor in Lebanon trained me to pray, "Lord, fill me with your Holy Spirit. I am ready to share about you; would you open the conversation?" This prayer asks God to move in our conversation with a Muslim friend. We can trust that God's sovereignty puts us in the right place at the right time. So relax in God's power, and don't panic. He is always on the throne. Jesus still has all the authority.

The following ideas will help you share with people with whom you already enjoy a relationship, those God has already put in your path or circle of influence. So build the relationship and ask God to open the conversation. This is not to denigrate other kinds of outreach, such as proclamation evangelism. These are also valid, but that is not what we are talking primarily about in this book.

With an understanding of some of the basic beliefs and rituals of Islam in place, here are thoughts to help you start good conversations with Muslims.

BEGIN WITH A GREETING

Always begin with a greeting. Always smile when you greet people. Try learning a greeting in Persian, French, or Uzbek—or just use English. Say hello and share your name; people will feel safe and welcomed. Try to use words that are familiar to Muslims, such as *salam*, which means "peace," a word used in many Persian countries. *Marhaba* is heavily used in the Middle East, from Turkey to Morocco, and it means "hello" or "welcome." Another is *assalamu alaikum*, which means "peace be upon you," a common greeting among Muslims.

ASK GOOD QUESTIONS

Ask about your Muslim friend's life and culture. Continuing conversations will open up more discussions about family, likes, and dislikes. This is the main way to find out about your friend. Don't assume anything—ask!

Here are some sample questions that might help:

What country are you from?

Tell me about your home country.

What did you like and dislike about growing up there?

How long have you been in this country?

What do you like about this country?

What did you like about being raised as a Muslim?

What was one difficult experience as a child?

Did you know any Christians growing up? What was your opinion of them?

How do you practice your religion? Which practices mean the most to you?

What holidays (or *eids*) do you participate in? What do they mean to you?

Why do you think there are different religions?

Who is Jesus, in your opinion? How did you learn this about Jesus?

What have you heard about Jesus? How do you know those statements are true?

Have you read the Injeel, the revelation of Jesus?

LISTEN TO ANSWERS

As we share the good news, it's imperative that we don't rush. Listen to your friend's answers, and ask God to give you discernment for your replies. Maybe your friend has been through a traumatic experience or has questions about Jesus and the Christian faith. Listening shows the other person respect and often gives opportunities to share the gospel that you wouldn't otherwise have.

After I spoke at a conference in Ohio, a Christian woman asked me how to share with a Somali neighbor who had fled for her life after seeing her own father tied to the bumper of a car and dragged along the street until he was dead. I encouraged her to listen closely to her friend's pain and then use the Bible to help her heal from this horrible trauma. We must *listen*.

STAY BIBLICAL

In Isaiah 55:11, God affirms that his word will not return void. Always be ready to share what the Bible says about a specific issue. Many Muslims enjoy hearing Bible verses read, for they may have never had access to the Bible. And some are grateful that the Bible deals with many of their unanswered questions concerning God, prophets, and the Messiah Jesus.

Many Muslims are refreshed as they hear of God's power and grace. Many say they like the details of the stories of the prophets. The parables of Jesus are effective tools to explain spiritual concepts. The Bible is a source for our Christian walk; when shared, it impacts Muslims. Much like adding potassium to water, a reaction always takes place.

One Muslim who became a believer in Christ told me that he appreciates the Bible because it focuses on principles and not rituals. Your friends may feel the same way.

EXPECT RESULTS

Finally, have faith that God will bring the results he desires. Faith is trust. Do you believe he can use you to lead a Muslim to Christ?

My first Christmas in the US as an international college student was in Cleveland. My roommate invited me to his home to enjoy the break. When he took me to visit the lakefront, the lake was frozen. My roommate told me that I could walk on the ice. Not experienced with such things, I protested that surely the ice would break. My roommate assured me that it wouldn't because the ice was thick enough to support us.

How much faith did I need to walk on this ice? If the ice were thin, it would break, and it wouldn't matter how much I believed in it. It isn't the amount of our faith that matters, but rather the trustworthiness and strength of whatever we trust.

So expect results and trust God as you begin your conversations. He will give you the courage and the wisdom to be his ambassador. Our faith is in "him who is able to do immeasurably more than all we ask or imagine, according to his power that is at work within us" (Eph. 3:20). Our faith has the strongest of all foundations.

55 Seconds for Change

Take a minute and think of a Muslim friend or acquaintance in your neighborhood or at your job. Think of anything you have in common and any possible points of connection (kids, hobbies, etc.). Thank the Lord Jesus for that precious person made in God's image. Ask the Lord Jesus to open the door to a genuine friendship between you.

I recommend this prayer:

God, you are the Lord of the universe. You seek to save the lost. I pray that you would bless [name of person/persons]. Please give them a seeking heart that is open to a conversation about Jesus and salvation. I am ready to share. Thank you for the gospel that changes lives. In Jesus's name I pray. Amen.

Chapter 11

FOCUSING OUR CONVERSATIONS

In *Seeking Allah, Finding Jesus*, Nabeel Qureshi shares a story from his tenth-grade year. A classmate asked Nabeel, who was a Muslim at the time, if he knew Jesus as Savior. She was the first Christian to ever ask him this. Nabeel wondered why other Christians had never raised the subject. Were they not concerned about his salvation? Or was it possible that Christians didn't believe their own faith?

What a sobering series of questions to us who are committed Christians. Why do we wait? Why do we avoid? Why do we not take the initiative? Why do we not focus our conversations?

Let's remember that there are three basic types of Muslims: cultural Muslims, devout Muslims, and converts to Islam. The approach I am presenting here can focus our conversations with any type of Muslim.

When talking with adherents of Islam, it's imperative that we start where *they* are, rather than from our own wording and ideas. It's easy to use terminology and spiritual concepts that *we* understand as followers of Jesus. Many of us have read the

Bible multiple times, and we're highly familiar with biblical concepts that Muslims have never heard. Muslims don't know, for example, the biblical concepts of grace, faith, redemption, and substitutionary death. They might have similar terminology, but the meaning is usually completely different.

Jesus was the master of the art of evangelism. He took the initiative and intentionally maneuvered his conversations to share the good news. Many passages in the Gospels help us see how Jesus effectively communicated the good news of salvation. We are to be like our Savior, who was strategic in his conversations to declare to all that he is truly the Savior of the world (John 4:42).

Going out of your way to interact with people who might otherwise not encounter another believer is key to reaching Muslims. Make the effort to be where they are: stores, refugee centers, universities, Muslim-majority countries. Ninety percent of Muslim ministry is just showing up in their lives and letting God do the rest. Remember that God cares about the souls of Muslims even more than we do.

Being willing to start conversations with others, to draw them out of their shells in a respectful, friendly way, is an important way to reach Muslims. Muslims often come from cultures that are hospitable, and many seek friendships in the countries to which they immigrate. Also, many are interested in spiritual conversations, especially as the Muslim world is torn by sectarian and geopolitical strife. Our ministry teams report weekly about the openness of Muslims when hearing the gospel.

In the Bible, our Messiah Jesus had a conversation with a Samaritan woman that led to her salvation and the salvation of her village (John 4). We see Christ initiating a conversation over a cup of water—something physical and basic. Begin your conversation with your friend's felt needs—whether emotional, physical, or social. It could begin over sports, business, politics, or even donated goods. Spiritual conversations don't have to begin on a spiritual topic; they usually begin with a tangible, concrete, day-to-day subject.

I've found it easy to open conversations with Muslims because, like the Samaritan woman, they already talk about their religion! It's natural for them. I just capitalize on the opportunities God presents. We need not fear opening an exchange about spiritual topics with Muslims, even if we're not in a religious setting.

FOCUS ON THE PERSON

Always begin with the person in mind. Pray for God to guide you. Ask him to fill you with the Holy Spirit.

Pray, "Lord, if you want me to share the gospel, you open the conversation." If you do, you may find yourself immediately responding to questions a Muslim has always had about Jesus and the Christian faith. Focus on those you are talking to. God will give you insights about their lives, right from the conversation. Are they refugees? Are they intellectual? Are they students? Are they professionals? Do they have family back in the home country? Do they have teenagers? Are they struggling with work, language, or loneliness?

Our Savior ministered to the whole person; let us be like him. First focus on your friend and then move the focus of the conversation to who Jesus is according to the Bible—there will be ample time to discuss details of social life later!

You may run into the argument that the Bible has been

corrupted, an idea I will respond to in later chapters. The goal of this chapter is simply to remember, as ambassadors of Jesus, to keep our conversation focused on the biblical teachings of Jesus.

FOCUS ON THE BIBLE

Jesus is mentioned in the Qur'an, but later we will see that the Jesus of Islam isn't the Jesus of the Qur'an, and the Jesus of the Qur'an isn't the Jesus of the Bible. So we must be committed to sharing the Jesus of the Bible. His question recorded in Matthew 16:15 echoes through the centuries: "Who do you say I am?"

There are numerous bridges to the gospel from the Qur'an. But the gospel isn't in the Qur'an—it's in the Bible. We must move the conversation to the biblical foundation of our faith. Muslims and Christians enjoy common ground, but if we dwell too long there, we will never move toward building bridges. From the beginning of the conversation, set your heart and mind on proclaiming the Jesus of the Bible.

Minister to the whole person. Is there a need to be met? A difficulty to pray for? A sickness or mental illness to address? Conversational apologetics introduces biblical answers to each situation. Let us not be distracted by political questions or Islamic propaganda. Focus on answers from the Bible.

What does the Bible say about war and peace? What does it say about godly conduct? Who is God, and why is Jesus the only Savior? Read biblical passages such as John 3; John 8–10; Romans 10; and Matthew 5–7.

Correcting misconceptions is another important way to focus on the Bible. Because of erroneous Islamic teachings across the Muslim world, many Muslims have misconceptions about

Jesus, the Bible, and Christianity. Many believe Christians worship three gods. Others think we believe there was a sexual act between God Almighty and the Virgin Mary. Others think we steal children and molest them. Others believe that all Christians hate all Muslims. Some think we are drunkards because America has so many beer commercials. Others sincerely want to lead us out of our "error" to join Islam.

Regardless of the misconception, the Word of God, called the sword of the Spirit (Eph. 6:17), is a mighty tool for answering all such errors. Listen to your friend and answer from the Word, focusing on our Savior, who said, "I am . . . the truth" (John 14:6).

One of the key goals in every conversation with our Muslim friends ought to be to interest them in the Bible so they will read the gospel for themselves. My friend Grace is a committed Christian. She once had a conversation about Jesus with a sweet, young, Muslim, shoe-store clerk. The young woman asked if Grace could pray for her. Grace said she would, and she inquired whether the store clerk was interested in a copy of the Injeel. This Sunni lady said yes, and two other workers (also Muslims) overheard the conversation and came forward to say they too wanted copies. Later Grace returned to the store and happily gave away three Arabic and English New Testaments.

God's Word is more powerful than our words, however eloquently or sincerely spoken. "The word of God is alive and active. Sharper than any double-edged sword, it penetrates even to dividing soul and spirit, joints and marrow; it judges the thoughts and attitudes of the heart" (Heb. 4:12). When we offer someone God's Word, we discover the wonderful truth that the Bible speaks for itself, keeping in mind that the Holy Spirit makes the words meaningful to the reader (John 14:26).

An imam from a Shia background entered a coffee shop to read and to wait for some friends he was visiting in the States. As he waited, an American Christian began a conversation with him and welcomed him to the state. That simple gesture of friendship initiated a series of conversations that led the imam to begin reading the Bible. Eventually he came to faith in Christ after reading these verses: "Watch out for false prophets. They come to you in sheep's clothing, but inwardly they are ferocious wolves. By their fruit you will recognize them. Do people pick grapes from thornbushes, or figs from thistles? Likewise, every good tree bears good fruit, but a bad tree bears bad fruit" (Matt. 7:15–17).

Similarly, Muhammad, a Syrian refugee, began talking with a Lebanese pastor. The conversation moved to the authenticity of the Bible, and Muhammad asked for an Arabic Bible. Soon Muhammad read these verses: "If you love those who love you, what reward will you get? Are not even the tax collectors doing that? And if you greet only your own people, what are you doing more than others? Do not even pagans do that? Be perfect, therefore, as your heavenly Father is perfect" (Matt 5:46–48). Convicted, Muhammad decided to be baptized and to follow Jesus. The Bible is indeed sharper than a double-edged sword.

55 Seconds for Change

You may be the only Christian a Muslim speaks with today. Ask God to connect you with a follower of Islam. Commit to focusing your conversation on the person, on Jesus, and on the Bible. Take the initiative! Then let God lead as you dispel misconceptions and shine the light of the gospel into your friend's heart and life. Here is a suggested prayer:

Father God, fill me with your Holy Spirit. I am ready to share the good news. Please open the conversations so that I can share your good news. In Jesus's name. Amen.

Chapter 12

STAYING ON MESSAGE

While I was visiting a friend from Algeria in a coffee shop, the owner struck up a conversation with both of us about Jesus. In typical Arab fashion, the conversation wasn't on a single topic. It moved from politics to culture to the economy, and finally to the Messiah Jesus.

In my experience, this situation is typical when sharing the gospel with Muslims. These conversations rarely stay focused on a clear understanding of the Christian faith. Often Muslims say, "Well, someone told me this," or, "A neighbor said that"—or perhaps someone shared with them the wrong biblical or qur'anic verse. When your conversation is over, you wonder if the message about the Lord got through.

As ambassadors for Christ, we have to stay on the main topic of the uniqueness of Jesus. The Great Commission is specifically about "teaching them to obey everything I have commanded you" (Matt. 28:20). Jesus is the way, the truth, and the life (John 14:6). That's the core message.

Staying on message isn't only important for clarity in evangelism but also to be good stewards of our time. As we discussed earlier, conversational apologetics are to bring the conversation back to the Savior. There are many topics to discuss. I might feel passionate about political or social issues. Nevertheless, my role is to go and make disciples and share what Christ taught. My conversation with my Muslim friend, whether short or long, should reflect the teachings of Jesus.

Muslims can read the whole Bible, the whole Qur'an, and the whole Hadith on the internet. God is using technology to make the truth more accessible, for he is powerful. And many resources today, from online media to books to audio materials, can assist in sharing the good news. These tools might be helpful in conveying a clearer message to our Muslim friends, and there is nothing wrong with them. But I want you to be able to speak with your Muslim friends without relying on those resources. Don't worry; you can do this!

Often our conversations fall short because we aren't able to move to the next point that clarifies the issue, and clarity is important in what we are asking Muslims to do—believe in Jesus as Lord and Savior. Ask them to believe in a deity? They already do. Believe in Jesus? They *think* they do. We are to be clear in our message and in the response Jesus requires.

The following is a basic mental outline that can help you, the evangelist, to keep your conversations on target.[9] Just remember this basic principle: *Always start with similarities, and then move into the gospel.*

1. GOD IS LOVE:
AL-WADUD

In the Bible, the creator of the universe seeks fellowship with his creation.

The Injeel says,

> "God is love. Whoever lives in love lives in God, and God
> in them." (1 John 4:16)

> "I [Jesus] have come that they may have life, and have it to
> the full." (John 10:10)

So why is our world so far from God? Why do people feel
separated from God?

2. GOD IS HOLY:
AL-QUDUS

We have all sinned against God Almighty and cannot remove
our guilt.

The Injeel affirms that all have sinned against a holy
God:

> "There is no one righteous, not even one;
>> there is no one who understands;
>> there is no one who seeks God.
> All have turned away,
>> they have together become worthless;
> there is no one who does good,
>> not even one." (Rom. 3:10–12)

> "All have sinned and fall short of the glory of God."
> (Rom. 3:23)

3. GOD IS JUST:
AL-ADIL

Sin separates us from our loving and holy God and results in spiritual death. The Injeel says, "The wages of sin is death" (Rom. 6:23).

4. GOD IS MERCIFUL:
AL-RAHEEM

Sin has created a gulf between us and God. Jesus Christ is the only bridge between a holy God and sinful humans.

The Injeel teaches, "There is salvation in no one else, for there is no other name under heaven given among men by which we must be saved" (Acts 4:12 ESV).

We must now ask, *Why Jesus and no one else?*

5. MIRACULOUS BIRTH

All prophets have claimed that they were just humans, while Jesus Christ claimed to be the Word of God, *Kalimat Allah*.

The Injeel tells us the story from the beginning of Jesus's earthly life:

> The angel said to her, "Do not be afraid, Mary; you have found favor with God. You will conceive and give birth to a son, and you are to call him Jesus. He will be great and will be called the Son of the Most High. The Lord God

will give him the throne of his father David, and he will reign over Jacob's descendants forever; his kingdom will never end."

"How will this be," Mary asked the angel, "since I am a virgin?"

The angel answered, "The Holy Spirit will come on you, and the power of the Most High will overshadow you. So the holy one to be born will be called the Son of God. Even Elizabeth your relative is going to have a child in her old age, and she who was said to be unable to conceive is in her sixth month." (Luke 1:30–36)

6. MIRACULOUS LIFE

Jesus Christ, who lived a sinless life of purity and honesty, was obedient to the laws of God, taught like no one else, and miraculously healed every weakness and disease he encountered.

Here's one example from the Injeel:

Jesus went throughout Galilee, teaching in their synagogues, proclaiming the good news of the kingdom, and healing every disease and sickness among the people. News about him spread all over Syria, and people brought to him all who were ill with various diseases, those suffering severe pain, the demon-possessed, those having seizures, and the paralyzed; and he healed them. Large crowds from Galilee, the Decapolis, Jerusalem, Judea and the region across the Jordan followed him. (Matt. 4:23–25)

7. MIRACULOUS DEATH

Jesus Christ came to be the sinless sacrifice of God and redeem humanity from its fallen state. The Injeel states, "Look, the Lamb of God, who takes away the sin of the world!" (John 1:29).

8. MIRACULOUS RESURRECTION

Christ rose from the dead on the third day, according to prophecy, proving that his sacrifice was acceptable to God.

The Injeel gives us this account:

> What I received I passed on to you as of first importance: that Christ died for our sins according to the Scriptures, that he was buried, that he was raised on the third day according to the Scriptures, and that he appeared to Cephas [Peter], and then to the Twelve. After that, he appeared to more than five hundred of the brothers and sisters at the same time, most of whom are still living, though some have fallen asleep. (1 Cor. 15:3–6)

9. GOD IS FORGIVING:
AL-GHAFOOR

It isn't enough to know that God has found an *Adha*, a redeemer, for sin; each of us needs to receive this sacrifice in a personal and humble decision.

The Injeel says, "The wages of sin is death, but the gift of God is eternal life in Christ Jesus our Lord" (Rom. 6:23).

10. GOD HEARS OUR PRAYERS

Prayer is talking to God. We can pray to God wherever we are and whenever we want. To receive Christ's sacrifice (the Christian *Adha*), we are to pray to God in faith (trusting God).

Your prayer to God might be something like this:

Dear Lord, thank you for your love for me. I ask your forgiveness earned by Christ's atoning death. I open the door of my life and receive Jesus Christ as my Lord and Savior. Make me a new person. Thank you for giving me eternal life. In Jesus's name. Amen.

Pray this and ask Christ to enter your life, forgive your sins, and restore your fellowship with God. If you sincerely asked Christ to enter your life, be assured that he did and that he will hold you fast.

As the Injeel promises that "he who began a good work in you will carry it on to completion until the day of Christ Jesus" (Phil. 1:6).

55 Seconds for Change

Whenever you talk about the good news of Jesus Christ, make sure you get to "the ask." Ask your Muslim friend if he or she would like to take Jesus as Savior and Lord. A favorite question: "What is the one thing stopping you from following Jesus?" Here are two more: "Would you like to become a follower of Jesus today?" "Would you like to have the assurance of going to heaven today?" Now ask God to give you the opportunity to speak with a Muslim about the Savior.

Chapter 13

HURDLES TO FOLLOWING JESUS

After speaking to a group of collegians in Toledo, Ohio, I was invited to have a cup of coffee with a Sunni Muslim student from Morocco. As we sat down, this computer science student said that Jesus was just a man and that Christians had corrupted and changed the Bible.

Before responding to these common objections, I wisely lifted up a silent prayer, asking God to help me clearly communicate the gospel of Jesus to this educated young man. I began speaking to him in my usual way about the uniqueness of Jesus, but he interrupted me with a question I had never heard before: "Fouad, aren't you afraid of genies?"

I stopped in my tracks. "What do you mean?"

"Aren't you afraid of genies appearing in the night and choking you to death?"

As it turned out, this engineer's grandfather was a village sheikh who was knee-deep in the occult. He would cast spells and chant the Qur'an to ward off genies (*jinn*) for villagers. While this young man's objections were important and deserved an answer, I might have missed the opportunity to connect if I hadn't discovered his most pressing felt need—his fear of the jinn.

THE BIGGEST HURDLES

In much the same way, the following hurdles must be cleared if we are to share the gospel effectively with Muslims. Later in the chapter we will look at sensitive ways to address such misconceptions. But for now, we need to understand that few Muslims fit the straightforward descriptions of them and their faith that we often see in religious surveys and textbooks.

Misinformation about Christianity

Today, even in our information age, millions of Muslims carry misconceptions about other religions, especially Christianity. Many have traditional but inaccurate information about both Islam and Christianity. Sadly, I commonly hear Muslims accuse Christians of idolatry, believing that we worship Mary and Jesus as separate gods. This teaching, of course, is blasphemy in all Christian denominations and sects.

Another critical mistake many Muslims believe is that the message of Jesus was incomplete. They think this is why Muhammad, the prophet of Islam, had to come. Others might want to read the Bible but don't because they believe it has been corrupted. Corruption, in their mind, is that the words of Jesus were not copied correctly and additional teachings were added to the Bible. This is the basic hurdle that must be addressed in the minds of Muslims. The Bible has to be seen as trustworthy so Muslims will consider its teachings on God, Jesus, and salvation.

Misinformation about the West

Although technology has made the globe seem smaller, many Muslims don't know a single practicing Christian. Few have Christian friends or neighbors, and this makes it hard for them to see a Christian community in action.

Also, Western media and entertainment paint a picture of Western culture (which Muslims generally view as *Christian* culture) as awash in immorality, vice, and impiety. Some media outlets ridicule the Savior Jesus and his teachings, confusing Muslims more: Why would a Christian culture ridicule its Savior?

Islamic Propaganda

Many Muslim governments work hand in hand with Islamic outreach movements to spread the Muslim faith. They hold community meetings describing what they see as Islam's superiority over other religions, they run advertisements on the benefits of sharia, and they regularly criticize the Christian faith.

Islamic propaganda is prevalent in Muslim countries, and it engulfs Muslims' daily lives, making it difficult for them to be critical thinkers about rituals and religions. The government also demands respect for the prophet. Muhammad's character or behavior can never be questioned. Some countries, such as Pakistan, have notorious blasphemy laws to control any discussion about Muhammad's life and teachings. Those who are found guilty of violating such laws usually face harsh penalties, not to mention social strictures.

The strictness of these laws is far from an academic issue. A Muslim teacher in Sudan asked the sheikh (imam) at his local mosque why Muslims are required to pray five times a day if

God can hear our prayers anytime. Simply for asking the question, this teacher was accused of blasphemy and subsequently beheaded. How tragic!

Political Pressure

Many Muslim countries make Islam their official religion, thus conflating religion and nationality and making conversion to any other religion illegal. In addition to anti-blasphemy laws, many Muslim-majority countries also have the death penalty for those who leave Islam. Access to the internet and outside media is limited, blocking opportunities for citizens to see or hear teachings from the Bible.

Religious Pressure

When a child is born in the Muslim world, a male elder must whisper the *shahadah* in his or her ear. Even if the family does not speak or understand Arabic, it has to be recited in Arabic. This act declares that the child is a Muslim. There are no other options.

A consistent theme in the Qur'an is that Allah loves only Muslims and accepts only the religion of Islam. It even says that God hates all non-Muslims and calls them *kafir* (blasphemers) and *mushrikeen* (idol worshipers). From childhood, Muslims are taught that other religions and their followers are inferior. Muslims are taught never to investigate these religions.

And what is Allah like? Islam is clear that God is transcendent, unknowable, impersonal, and much like a cosmic force. God has a name in the Qur'an, and it's the Arabic word *Allah*. Allah of the Qur'an is the source not only of good but also of evil. He created Satan to torment humans and sin to test humanity. Allah is neither predictable nor dependable. He can change his mind on Judgment Day, creating fear and uncertainty in the hearts of millions of Muslims.

In a very real sense, Islam portrays humans as slaves and Allah as the master. Allah in Islam demands total obedience. In contrast, Jesus claimed that God is the heavenly Father, and humans are invited to become his children (John 1:12).

Merit and Salvation

Many Muslims argue the benefits of good works to attain salvation. The blessings of Allah are called *baraka*, and Muslims seek these for themselves and for their families and communities. So it was a shock when a terrible tsunami hit Banda Aceh, Indonesia's most religious and Islamic area, in 2004. If Allah can be counted on to consistently reward good works in this life, how could such a catastrophe happen?

The uncertainty over what Allah may do causes many Muslims to live in fear, not sure if they have done enough good works to receive the *baraka*. Because they fear their actions might bring on the wrath of an unpredictable, implacable God, they avoid investigating the claims of the Bible.

Social Pressure and Shaming

In most Muslim-majority countries, non-Muslim minorities receive harsh or unfair treatment, while followers of Islam receive full rights. This creates another huge pressure on Muslims not to consider investigating the claims of Christ. Why lose all these privileges? Why consider a religion of second-class citizens? Why would they need to investigate a religion that Islam has already replaced (because Islam came after Christianity)?

The concept of shame and honor is found in every thread

of a Muslim society's social fabric, in everything from how a person uses a toothpick to asking questions about life and religion. This approach to life exerts serious pressure on anyone contemplating a change of faith.

People growing up in the Middle East hear statements such as these: "It's shameful to question the imam!" "These questions about the Qur'an are *haram* (sinful, shameful)." "Your daughter should wear the hijab—shame on her for not wearing it!" The social pressure to appease the family and the community can become so great that many people are too frightened to investigate any other religions. Leaving Islam might very well mean leaving the community. How many of us would consider doing that?

This social pressure can create a spirit of religious competition among Muslims that would invite the envy of the ancient Pharisees. Muslims across the Muslim world who keep the five daily prayer times develop a mark on their forehead. That mark comes from hitting one's head on the carpet multiple times a day in the fashion of Muslim prayer. Men who develop this mark walk in the streets making sure all see it. This mark is called the *zebibah*, meaning "raisin," since the affected skin becomes a little darker.

OVERCOMING THE HURDLES

We must understand these oft-unstated hurdles as we speak with Muslims about Jesus. Muslims need our help to overcome them. They need the power of God's Spirit to convict and convince them. Let us address these hurdles as we reason with our Muslim friends about the faith. I have two primary ways of doing this.

Use the Bible

Our responses must be biblical. A Muslim once asked me about polygamy. He claimed it's the solution for adultery. I could have argued with him about the rather dubious merits of this claim, and I would have been justified in doing so. After all, women are not pawns in a game called marriage, run by the whims of men. Instead, I answered him from Scripture: the Bible commands me to love my wife just as Jesus loved the church (Eph. 5:25). This response had a lot more effect on my friend because it was powered by the living and active Word of God (Heb. 4:12). The Bible is our guide in all matters of faith and conduct, and we need to share that information with our Muslim friends.

The Bible also gives many answers to the specific hurdles they face. Regarding family pressure, for instance, John 1:12 declares that if we are a child of God, then we are in a new family made up of all nations. This was a comfort to an Afghan, Muslim-background believer I met, as she understood that her family is now global.

The Bible further declares that believers are citizens of heaven and Jesus is our ruler. In Revelation 7:9 we see an international celebration around God's throne. Believers may face political pressures in this world, but the kingdom of God is not controlled by a political leader or religious group. Christians are to obey the laws of our various countries, influence their neighbors toward biblical values, and pray for their leaders (1 Tim. 2:1–4), but the Bible is clear that we belong to another kingdom.

Jesus has set us free from sin and condemnation. Merit is not a part of our salvation. This is such a refreshing conviction; it can make new Muslim-background believers leap with joy and assurance. They are saved, cleansed, and assured of forgiveness by the redemption of Christ.

Focus the Conversation on Following Jesus

Humanity's greatest need is the Savior Jesus. When sharing your faith, avoid political conversations, which lead to strife. Jesus is the only cure for the sins and injustices of this world. Don't ask Muslims to exchange one religious ritual for another. Faith isn't about works, piety, and religious actions. It's about taking Jesus as one's Savior. Let's focus on our need for the Savior to redeem us from our sins.

Let's also remember that the life of Christ is a powerful source for continual spiritual growth. Unapologetically tell your Muslim friends that Jesus the Messiah came to defeat the works of the devil, including our fear and anxiety. A Muslim-background believer named Husam, after reading the biblical command not to be ashamed of Jesus (Mark 8:38), shared his faith every day. Jesus defeated Satan, sin, and the grave. Jesus promises that no one can snatch us out of his hand (John 10:28). Our Messiah calmed the storm, walked on water, opened the eyes of the blind, and raised people from the dead.

55 Seconds for Change

What are some of the unstated hurdles in your culture and community that might keep Muslims from following Jesus? Write as many as you can think of. Ask other followers of Christ to share what other hurdles they see in your community. Seek to present solutions based on a biblical foundation. What Bible verses can help dispel these hurdles? What steps can the community take to alleviate these pressures? Ask God to give you insight and empathy as you work with Muslims. Especially in shame-based cultures, many carry a heavy burden of low self-esteem and shame.

Abba, Father, your Son came to take our shame from us. I have been set free from the guilt and shame of my sin. Help me be a source of comfort and guidance to my Muslim neighbors and friends. May your peace shine through me and help them overcome hurdles and follow Jesus the Savior. In his name. Amen.

Part 3

CONVERSATIONAL
APOLOGETICS

Chapter 14

THE MAIN THING

One day a Sunni man from Turkey asked his neighbor, a Christian pastor, "Why do Christians eat fish and bread every Sunday?"

The question surprised the pastor. He responded, "Well, it's actually bread and wine for communion—why do you think it's bread and fish?"

"When I was a young teenager," the Muslim replied, "I visited a Catholic church in Istanbul, where I saw a painting of Jesus holding a basket of fish and a basket of bread. It seemed that Christians favor fish and bread in their Sunday meals."

This exchange launched a wonderful conversation about the uniqueness of Jesus. The Turkish man is now studying the Bible with his neighbor.

Any honest question, however small it may seem, can lead to sharing the whole gospel. I love hearing testimonies of Muslim-background believers in Christ. One simple question can lead to a deep conversation about the Savior Jesus.

There's a special art to weaving the gospel through our conversations. Here we'll explore some practical ways to guide conversations toward the theological and spiritual issues behind the questions and objections of Muslims.

As ambassadors for Christ, we need to be ready to respond to issues and questions others might raise. The answers to these important questions show the relevance of the Christian faith and are an important part of what we call apologetics.

Apologetics comes from the Greek word *apologia*. It denotes a defense, not an apology. It's not that we apologize for or are embarrassed by Christian teachings; rather, we present a logical defense of the Christian faith. This process fits with how God created us as logical creatures. In the Bible God communicates directly to our logic and intellect. In the book of Acts, for example, we see the disciples of Jesus going into the streets, theaters, and synagogues, reasoning with people on the uniqueness of the Messiah Jesus.

Conversational apologetics will provide you with practical ways to explain biblical concepts to your Muslim friends. The ideas provided here can help you impart these concepts with ease, creating an environment of respect and openness.

As we will see later in this book, apologetics and reasoning aren't enough to lead a person to Christ, but they are necessary. No matter how airtight our defense of the Christian faith seems to be, we need the work of the Spirit to reveal God to people through signs, situations, and other means.

A colleague and I were in Michigan, and we met with an Arab Muslim couple. They were interested in knowing more about the Christian faith. The husband asserted that if we answered all his questions, he would consider becoming a Christian. We explained the gospel to him and answered every question he presented to us. At the end of our time together, my colleague asked him, "Are you ready to become a Christian?" The answer was no. That's because no amount of head knowledge will ever impel someone to cross the threshold of faith. Only the Holy Spirit can do that.

THE BIBLICAL MANDATE FOR APOLOGETICS

Biblical apologetics is based on the biblical mandate in 1 Peter 3:15–16: "In your hearts revere Christ as Lord. Always be prepared to give an answer to everyone who asks you to give the reason for the hope that you have. But do this with gentleness and respect, keeping a clear conscience, so that those who speak maliciously against your good behavior in Christ may be ashamed of their slander."

Let's look a little closer at these verses.

Set Apart Christ as Lord

The first Greek word we will examine is pronounced *kurios*: "lord," or "master." Is Jesus Christ the Lord of your life? Do you acknowledge him as the Lord of this moment? He must be the Lord of any conversation with a Muslim. This is the foundation as we embark on conversational apologetics. *Christ is with you.* Give him your words and attitudes.

God is actively involved on this planet. Regardless of what we see around us, the moment you meet a Muslim, remember that Christ is Lord. He has arranged this moment for you to be a witness.

Always Be Prepared

Since Matthew 28:18–20 declares that we go in the authority of Jesus, it is our responsibility to be prepared to share and testify.

To be prepared is to anticipate what will happen. It's like going on a hike in the mountains. You must predict hurdles, challenges, and achievements. You must purchase the proper equipment and make sure you have a way to get to the trail. You must plan for nourishment and shelter. You must also prepare for those wonderful moments when you are taking pictures from the top of the mountain.

Likewise, you need to be prepared for a full conversation with your Muslim friend. We have already discussed your spiritual position and your attitudes. These approaches will help prepare you for the conversation. Always show expectancy for what God will do. *Always be prepared* means you know that in some conversations you are either planting a seed, watering a seed, or harvesting. But no matter the conversation, its topic or length, Jesus is the Lord of every word that passes between you.

And finally you must be ready to insert apt biblical concepts and verses to bless your Muslim friend.

Give an Answer

The Greek word translated for "answer" is *apologia*, which can also mean a defense, the reasoning behind a certain attitude, or a course of action. The beauty of this verse is that we are to be prepared always to give a *defense*.

When we give answers to questions posed by our Muslim friends, we are defending the faith. As we have seen, Muslims today have much misinformation about Jesus, the Bible, and the Christian faith. Unfortunately, many Muslims are afraid to ask questions in their community and family. They are never supposed to question their leaders, Islamic teachings, or the Qur'an. So be patient in answering their questions. The *apologia*, the defense, means answering the questions with which Muslims are grappling.

Everyone Who Asks

Contrary to common perception, millions of Muslims are searching for the Savior Jesus. Men and women across the Islamic world are asking questions because of all the social change, civil wars, and refugee crises they are experiencing. This is a new awakening, unlike any in the past. Many Muslims want to know what we believe about God, heaven, and even social relationships.

These verses from 1 Peter are powerful, for they put us in a posture of *expectancy*: be ready to answer whoever asks. It also puts us in a posture of *faith*, for God is moving in the hearts of Muslims prior to our reasoning with them about the gospel. It also puts us in a posture of *gathering*; we are finding the lost sheep of the Savior.

So don't fret or worry, for Jesus is building his church.

Reason for Our Hope

The purpose of our conversations isn't to win an argument or merely to impart interesting information—though there is nothing more interesting than the good news! We are to focus our conversation on Jesus and his redemption. When we do this, we are keeping the main thing the main thing. In this part of the text, God tells us to give a reason. Remember, even God reasons with the human mind to demonstrate his holiness by offering salvation to all.

> "Come now, let us reason together,"
>   says the LORD.
> "Though your sins are like scarlet,
>   they shall be as white as snow;
> though they are red as crimson,
>   they shall be like wool." (Isa. 1:18 NIV 1984)

Our role is to answer questions and lead conversations that point to the redemption of humanity and those we speak with. History proves that mere religion does not change people; only Jesus can. Our every answer must reason with the Muslim mind. Our every answer must point to our hope in the redemption of Jesus.

In Gentleness and Respect

It's easy to lose heart or temper; it's easy to feel frustrated in one conversation after another. Sometimes you think it's going nowhere; maybe this person isn't listening.

This part of the text reminds us at such times that our posture should be gentle, which means kind. Be kind . . . and listen. Empathy is a great way to build acceptance and friendship. Many Muslims might be afraid of your reaction or opinion. Let us emulate our Savior Jesus, who delighted to welcome others.

This Bible passage also says to conduct ourselves with *respect*. Let's face it: it's easy to be judgmental as we see people living without the true God. But we are to be respectful, not condescending or superior. It's easy to ridicule other people's rituals and beliefs. The Bible does not ask us to agree with everybody—simply to listen and to respond with reason, in gentleness and respect.

WHAT'S AHEAD

This section (part 3) of the book is filled with examples of conversational apologetics in action. Each chapter begins with a question that frequently comes up in conversations with Muslims. We will look at the Qur'an and Islamic teachings. We'll compare them with what the Bible says. Then we'll include specific principles for sharing the reason for the hope within us.

Remember:

- Conversational apologetics isn't about a mental exercise or a battle of wits.
- Conversational apologetics isn't about ridiculing or insulting one's listeners.
- Conversational apologetics isn't a tool to elevate oneself or show one's superior logic and intellect.

No, conversational apologetics is a simple way to steer the conversation to the main issue: the hope that is within us—Jesus of Nazareth, the Messiah.

Conversational apologetics demands that we answer the questions and issues presented to us and lead the conversation back to Christ. It uses other people's questions as a platform to present Christ as the hope of all creation.

Conversational apologetics refines the conversation to be gentle and respectful while being truthful about the uniqueness of Jesus, his life, his teachings, and his resurrection from the dead. Biblical apologetics keeps Jesus as the main issue.

When I've engaged in conversational apologetics, I've seen God move in ways that I never would have expected. One hot day in southern Spain, I was speaking with a Moroccan young man named Khalid who claimed that the Injeel has been corrupted. I wanted to go into answering the question but instead felt compelled to share my testimony. He was so touched by how Christ saved me from hate and anger that the conversation concluded with him taking a Bible. His comment: "Fouad, you have found the cure for sin in the Bible—I want to find it too."

55 Seconds for Change

Always share your testimony of what Jesus has done for you—that is, tell your story. You are the only one who owns *that* narrative, and no one can challenge your personal experience. Though you may be describing what's happened to *you*, this is truly the best way to keep the focus on *Jesus*. We'll dig more into how to prepare your testimony, but for right now jot down your thoughts in answer to this question: *Who is Jesus to you?*

What was your life like before you met Jesus? What prompted you to start wondering if he might be calling you? Why did you turn to him? How has your life changed so far because of Jesus? Your answers will speak louder than anything else you can say.

God has changed you; can he not change the one you share with?

Chapter 15

THE TRINITY

On a train ride from Casablanca to Marrakesh, I spoke with a high school student. He said to me in the middle of our conversation, "Christians are *kafir* [blasphemers, unbelievers, atheists] because they worship three gods."

When I asked this young man to explain, he stated with utter confidence that Christians worship God the Father, Mary the mother, and Jesus the Son." He then asked, "Why do Christians worship three gods, while Muslims worship only one?"

How can we respond to this question? The answer is vital if we're to overcome this hurdle in the minds of our Muslim friends and lead them to a real encounter with the Savior.

In this chapter we will address this issue in the following sequence: (1) qur'anic references to the Trinity, (2) Islamic thought on the subject and the impact this has on the daily lives of Muslims, (3) the biblical foundation for the Trinity (the Christian position), and (4) how to use conversational apologetics to lead Muslims to the truth of the Bible. Throughout, keep in mind that God's nature is divine; it's above all reason. It isn't *against* all reason, but it's *above* all reason.

WHAT DOES THE QUR'AN SAY ABOUT THE TRINITY?

The Qur'an is clear that God is one—that no one and nothing is above him.

> Say, O Prophet, "How can you worship besides Allah those who can neither harm nor benefit you? And Allah alone is the All-Hearing, All-Knowing." (Qur'an 5:76)

> Say, O Prophet, "He is Allah—One and Indivisible; Allah—the Sustainer needed by all. He has never had offspring, nor was He born. And there is none comparable to Him." (Qur'an 112:1–4)

To give anything equal status with God is to commit *shirk*, an act of idolatry. It's unacceptable to give any lesser person or thing this kind of honor. One of the commonly quoted verses from the Qur'an that mentions the word *Trinity* is Qur'an 4:171:

> O People of the Book! Do not go to extremes regarding your faith; say nothing about Allah except the truth. The Messiah, Jesus, son of Mary, was no more than a messenger of Allah and the fulfilment of His Word through Mary and a spirit created by a command from Him. So believe in Allah and His messengers and do not say, "Trinity." Stop!—for your own good. Allah is only One God. Glory be to Him! He is far above having a son! To Him belongs whatever is in the heavens and whatever is on the earth. And Allah is sufficient as a Trustee of Affairs.

Does this verse have the same meaning in the original Arabic, though? No, it does not. This English translation uses the word *Trinity*. However, the original Arabic wording isn't *Trinity*, but *three gods*. The English translator used the word *Trinity*; but the Qur'an is warning people against worshiping three gods, namely, mistakenly worshiping God, Jesus, and Mary.

The Injeel is clear: there is one God, and Jesus is his word made flesh (John 1:1).

When Muslims think of the term *Trinity*, they think it means one of three things: that Christians worship more than one God, which is polytheism; that Christians worship humans on a level with God, which is idolatry; or that Christians say that God had a child with a human, which is blasphemous, resulting in a demigod. All these ideas are offensive to Christians as well as Muslims. It's important to understand that the Christian concept of the Trinity does not refer to idolatry, polytheism, or blasphemy; it's something else entirely.

Because of verses such as Qur'an 4:171 and the accusation by Muslim religious leaders that Christians worship three gods, it has been common among some Muslims to call Christians polytheists. Throughout Muslim history, Christian communities have been attacked as infidels and *mushrikeen*.

This misunderstanding of the Trinity leads Muslims to say that Christians should join Islam to save them from idolatry. Others claim that we naively worship three gods since, after all, 1 + 1 + 1 = 3. Criticism of the Trinity also gives Muslims a feeling of superiority, claiming Islam is monotheistic, while Christians are idol worshipers.

So when speaking with Muslims, address this topic as soon

as it comes up. Address it by indicating that Trinity has been revealed to us throughout the Bible, over many centuries and through different authors, under the guidance of divine inspiration. From Genesis onward, we see God, his Word, and his Spirit existing together and functioning in unison.

Al-tawheed in Islam means "the oneness of God." Muslims say they worship one God—not three, not four, not five—and the oneness of God. In Christianity there is also al-tawheed, but this is a complex "one," not a simple "one."

To gain a clearer understanding of what Christians mean when we talk about the Trinity, it's important to review what the Injeel says about the character of God: God the Creator, God the Redeemer, and God the Counselor.

WHAT DOES THE INJEEL SAY ABOUT THE TRINITY?

In the Injeel, the references to God as a Trinity are numerous and clear.

The Trinity Includes God the Father, Jesus the Son, and the Holy Spirit

> Then Jesus came to them and said, "All authority in heaven and on earth has been given to me. Therefore go and make disciples of all nations, baptizing them in the name of the Father and of the Son and of the Holy Spirit, and teaching them to obey everything I have commanded you. And surely I am with you always, to the very end of the age."
>
> —MATTHEW 28:18–20

Whoever Has Seen Jesus Has Seen God

> *Jesus answered: "Don't you know me, Philip, even after I have been among you such a long time? Anyone who has seen me has seen the Father. How can you say, 'Show us the Father'? . . .*
>
> *. . . "I will ask the Father, and he will give you another advocate to help you and be with you forever—the Spirit of truth."*
> —JOHN 14:9, 16–17

God's Holy Spirit Speaks Truth from God

> *"When he, the Spirit of truth, comes, he will guide you into all the truth. He will not speak on his own; he will speak only what he hears, and he will tell you what is yet to come."*
> —JOHN 16:13

The Injeel clearly teaches that the Holy Spirit speaks truth from God. There is no difference between any of the three persons of God. The idea of multiple aspects of God is visible even in the first book of the Tawrat (the Arabic name for the Torah, believed to be a holy book in the context of Islam).

God Uses Us and Our to Refer to the Trinity

> *Then God said, "Let us make mankind in our image, in our likeness."*
> —GENESIS 1:26

We can see from this verse that God uses *us* when he is talking. He does this because he is a Trinity, three persons in one. But who is the *us*? Who is included in the Trinity?

Though all Christians highly honor Mary the mother of Jesus, Christians do not believe Mary is part of the Trinity. Nor is there any place in the Injeel that says Mary is part of the Trinity. Christians believe that God always existed with his Word and Spirit. The Word of God was born in a manger, taking on human flesh as Jesus; therefore, the Trinity is the union of God the Father, Jesus, and the Holy Spirit. This subject, though clearly taught in the Bible, is nevertheless a subtle one, difficult even for Christians to grasp. It is no wonder, then, that Muslims have a hard time with it!

In the Injeel, we see an account of Jesus being baptized in the Jordan River (Matt. 3:16–17): "As soon as Jesus was baptized, he went up out of the water. At that moment heaven was opened, and he saw the Spirit of God descending like a dove and alighting on him. And a voice from heaven said, 'This is my Son, whom I love; with him I am well pleased.'"

During his baptism, the three persons of the Trinity are clearly revealed: God in the voice speaking from heaven; Jesus in the flesh on earth; and the Holy Spirit, descending.

GOD IN THREE PERSONS

But if God is one, as Muslims say, how can we understand the three persons of the Trinity? Let's look at those three persons in the Bible: God the Father, God the Son, and God the Holy Spirit.

God the Father

The first aspect of God that is usually listed in a description of the Trinity is God, also known as God the Father. The Tawrat, Zabur, and Injeel offer many pictures of God. God is good and generous (Ps. 84:11), great and sovereign (Ps. 99:1), and righteous and just (Ps. 37:28). God has many names that describe what he is like. God is El Elyon, God Most High (Isa. 14:13–15); Yahweh Yireh, the Lord Will Provide (Gen. 22:13–14); Yahweh Shalom, the Lord Is Peace (Judg. 6:24); El Olam, the Everlasting God (Isa. 40:28–31).[10]

God's character is revealed not only in his names but also in his actions. The names of God in the Bible are derived from a plethora of miracles and revelations. We see that he answers prayers throughout the Injeel, including the prayers of Jesus, the second person in the Trinity.

God is glorified when Jesus is glorified (John 17:1). God speaks to Jesus's disciples (Luke 9:34–35).

God the Son

Who is Jesus? According to the Bible, Jesus is a prophet (Luke 24:19), God's Son (Matt. 16:16), and the Word of God (John 1:1, 14). We see also that he often prayed to God as Father (Luke 23:34) and spoke of a third person in the Trinity, the Holy Spirit (John 14:16–17).

God the Holy Spirit

The Holy Spirit is the third person of the Trinity. What does the Injeel say about the Holy Spirit? The Holy Spirit is the spirit of God (1 Cor. 2:11; John 3:34), existed since before the beginning (Gen. 1:2), gives power (Acts 1:8), guides one's words (Matt. 10:19–20), performs miracles (Acts 2:4), and intercedes for believers (Rom. 8:26–27). In the Bible, people were acknowledged to be followers of God when the Holy Spirit was evident in their lives. The Holy Spirit comes to all who believe (Acts 10:44–46) and helps us to do good (Gal. 5:22–23).

55 Seconds for Change

The concept of God as Trinity may be above human reason, as we can never fully comprehend it in this life. But it is not *against* reason. Here's an idea to help your Muslim friend to at least see the plausibility of the Trinity. When you are confronted with questions or concerns about the Trinity, respond with a question of your own: "Who existed first? God, his Word, or his Spirit?"

Sometimes Muslims will quickly answer, "Oh, God existed first!" But this would mean he existed without his Word or his Spirit. That's impossible!

This question may help your friend to see that God the Father, from the beginning of time to the end of time, has always existed with his Word (God the Son) and with his Spirit (God the Holy Spirit).[11]

Chapter 16

MORE THAN A MAN
OR PROPHET

———————

Some years ago I led a Bible study in Arabic at the home of a friend from Syria. The house was filled with guests from different Arab countries: Lebanon, Syria, Iraq, Jordan, and Egypt.

It was a joy to open the Bible and read the story of Jesus healing the paralyzed man after forgiving his sins in Luke 5:17–26. Abdu, a young man from Iraq, listened intently. I asked him whether a prophet, a mere man, can forgive sins.

He said, "No! No human could do such a thing. Only God forgives sins!"

"But Jesus forgave sins," I replied.

Abdu said, "I've been reading the Bible, and I believe Jesus is more than a prophet."

That night, he committed his life to following Christ.

Muslims today are taught that they should love and respect Jesus, who is considered a prophet in Islam. They even agree with Christians on the virgin birth. But, unlike my friend Abdu, they believe he was, at the end of the story, just a man and not divine. How can we respond? What proof do we have that Jesus is more than a man?

THE QUR'ANIC RECORD: JESUS

What does the Qur'an say about *Isa bin Maryam* (Jesus, son of Mary)?

- Jesus, son of Mary, is the Christ (the Messiah).
  Remember when the angels proclaimed, "O Mary! Allah gives you good news of a Word from Him, his name will be the Messiah, Jesus, son of Mary; honoured in this world and the Hereafter, and he will be one of those nearest to Allah. (Qur'an 3:45)

- Mary, Jesus's mother, was a virgin.
  Mary wondered, "My Lord! How can I have a child when no man has ever touched me?" An angel replied, "So will it be. Allah creates what He wills. When He decrees a matter, He simply tells it, 'Be!' And it is!" (Qur'an 3:47)

- Jesus is a prophet.
  Say, O believers, "We believe in Allah and what has been revealed to us; and what was revealed to Abraham, Ishmael, Isaac, Jacob, and his descendants; and what was given to Moses, Jesus, and other prophets from their Lord. We make no distinction between any of them. And to Allah we all submit." (Qur'an 2:136)

Then in the footsteps of these prophets, We sent Our messengers, and after them We sent Jesus, son of Mary, and granted him the Gospel, and instilled compassion and mercy into the hearts of his followers. As for monasticism, they made it up—We never ordained it for them—only seeking to please Allah, yet they did not even observe it strictly. So We rewarded those of them who were faithful. But most of them are rebellious. (Qur'an 57:27)

- Jesus is in heaven with God.

  Rather, Allah raised him up to Himself. And Allah is Almighty, All-Wise. (Qur'an 4:158)

- Jesus is pure and sinless.

  He responded, "I am only a messenger from your Lord, sent to bless you with a pure son." (Qur'an 19:19)

- Jesus is the Word of God.

  O People of the Book! Do not go to extremes regarding your faith; say nothing about Allah except the truth. The Messiah, Jesus, son of Mary, was no more than a messenger of Allah and the fulfilment of His Word through Mary and a spirit created by a command from Him. So believe in Allah and His messengers and do not say, "Trinity." Stop!—for your own good. Allah is only One God. Glory be to Him! He is far above having a son! To Him belongs whatever is in the heavens and whatever is on the earth. And Allah is sufficient as a Trustee of Affairs. (Qur'an 4:171)

- Jesus would be born, die, and rise from the dead.

  Remember when Allah said, "O Jesus! I will take you and raise you up to Myself. I will deliver you from those who disbelieve, and elevate your followers above the disbelievers until the Day of Judgment. Then to Me you will all return, and I will settle all your disputes. (Qur'an 3:55)

  Peace be upon him the day he was born, and the day of his death, and the day he will be raised back to life! (Qur'an 19:15)

Muslims claim that Jesus is a respected prophet, and he is one of the *Ulul-azm* (an Arabic Islamic term given to special messengers sent by God, namely Adam, Noah, Abraham, Moses, and Jesus, with Muhammad as the final prophet). But is Jesus in Islam the same Jesus mentioned in the Bible? Is he the same Jesus whom millions of Christians, worship, revere, and follow?

Sadly, no.

Islam claims that Jesus came to prepare the way for Muhammad—that he prophesied the coming of another prophet whose name is Ahmad (meaning "most praised" or "commendable"), whom all must obey. Jesus was like all other prophets sent by God to lead people to worship the one God by facing Mecca and performing *salat* five times a day.

Islam further claims that Allah miraculously took Jesus to heaven in his physical body and had someone else crucified instead.

Finally, Islam claims that Jesus is returning at the end of the age to destroy churches—and specifically the crosses of the churches—and usher in an Islamic golden age ruled by the *Mahdi*, a spiritual and earthly leader who will restore religion and justice before the end of the world.

In all this, imams and other Muslim religious leaders generally explain the Christian faith and the teachings of Jesus from *their* point of view. They dismiss Christian worship of Jesus as the Son of God as idolatry, often accusing Christians of believing that Jesus is half human and half divine, denying the orthodox Christian doctrine of the hypostatic union, which holds that Jesus is fully God and fully man. Other Muslims believe Jesus is the result of a sexual union between God and Mary (*astaghfirullah*). God forbid!

THE UNIQUENESS OF JESUS

Both statements about Jesus's human and divine nature tragically misunderstand the doctrine of the virgin birth, and both are considered blasphemy in the Christian faith. Christians, as they engage in apologetics, need to highlight the broader implications of Jesus's virgin birth, including how it substantiates his identity as the Son of God. We believe this miracle proclaims the uniqueness of Christ. The angel answered, "The Holy Spirit will come on you, and the power of the Most High will overshadow you. So the holy one to be born will be called the Son of God" (Luke 1:35).

We agree that Jesus was also a prophet—but much more than merely a human prophet. The Bible claims that Jesus was the greatest prophet of all (Luke 24:19–21; John 8:58–59; 1 Tim. 2:5). And unlike any other prophet or religious leader in world history, Christ rose from the dead, victorious over sin and Satan.

(Read these Bible passages for the full story: Matthew 26–28; Mark 14–16; Luke 22–24; John 18–21; Acts 4:33; Romans 1:4; Romans 10:9–10; and 1 Peter 1:3.)

No doubt Islam has gotten some things right about Jesus, but it completely misses the mark about who he is. Muslims are misinformed about Jesus, his life, his character, and his teachings. Jesus is greater than any prophet because he is the Word of God incarnate and because he performed miracles, including the greatest miracle of all—rising from the dead. Millions of Muslims don't know that Jesus came to save them from their sin. Yet many are open to hearing more.

55 Seconds for Change

When you speak to your Muslim friends about this subject, use questions to help them understand the biblical position. Asking questions in a posture of respect builds trust and clears up confusion. The following questions are good tools to help your Muslim friend ponder the uniqueness of Jesus among all prophets:

- Why was Jesus born of the Virgin Mary? Why did no other prophet have such an amazing birth?
- Can a mere man raise the dead? Jesus had the power to raise the dead (Luke 7:11-17).
- Can a mere man walk on water, stop the storms, and know the thoughts of people around him?
- Can a mere man predict his own resurrection?
- What glorifies God more: to help Jesus to *escape* death or to *conquer* death?

These questions, asked in a spirit of love and respect, will enhance the conversation on the uniqueness of Jesus. Remember to stay in a spirit of prayer for God to reveal truth to your Muslim friend.

Chapter 17

WHO IS JESUS?

At a gathering of international students from Muslim countries, I had the privilege of speaking about the parable of the wise and foolish maidens in Matthew 25:1–13. I asked the students to read the text and discuss it around their tables.

The first question I asked was: *According to Jesus, Judgment Day resembles what kind of human activity?* They all agreed that it resembled a wedding in a village or small town. Right then, the room became a boisterous cultural competition over who has the best weddings, the Omanis or the Jordanians, the Saudis or the Persians, or perhaps the Turkish people. The banter was friendly as the room of over a hundred students came to life.

Then I asked a second question: *According to Jesus, is Judgment Day a happy day or a sad one?* The students were silent as they considered the issue. Then, in the middle of the silence, a young Ismaili Muslim from Kenya broke the silence. "Mr. Masri," he said. "It depends! Are you ready or not?"

Immediately I posed a third question: *If Judgment Day happened tonight, are you prepared to go to heaven?* The room again fell silent. The meeting was over, but conversations about salvation flourished. I was able to share the gospel clearly that night and in the days to follow.

Jesus is unique. There is none like this One who claims to be the coming Judge. But as I've shown, Muslims haven't been told that; they labor under many misconceptions handed down to them over the years and presented in the Qur'an. How can we lovingly help Muslims to see the truth of Jesus's greatness?

In the previous chapter, we saw that Jesus was more than a man. In this one we'll dig deeper by focusing on who Jesus is in the Bible. Along the way we'll learn how to present the Bible's teaching about the Lord to our Muslim friends.

WHAT DOES THE INJEEL SAY ABOUT JESUS?

The Bible emphasizes Jesus's miraculous birth, life, and resurrection. The Injeel says that Mary was a virgin when she gave birth to Jesus, a miracle of God, unlike anything that had ever happened before. Jesus then did many miracles in his lifetime through God's power. He healed people and taught them the truth, telling them what God led him to say. Jesus was killed unjustly, having committed no crime; but God raised him to life again. Jesus then ascended into heaven to be with God.

What follows are the key points of this divine story, along with appropriate verses that I encourage you to look up and meditate on in your Bible. Learn them, and you will be prepared to give an answer to every Muslim who asks you about Christ, with gentleness and respect!

Jesus, son of Mary, . . .

- is the Messiah (Matt. 1:16)
- was born of the Virgin Mary (Matt. 1:23; Luke 1:31–32)
- fulfills prophecy (Ps. 86:13; Isa. 53:11; Luke 2:6–7; John 1:36)
- is the Son of Man (Matt. 20:28; John 10:17–18)
- is the Son of God (Matt. 16:15–17; John 8:58; Col. 1:15)
- is Lord of creation (Matt. 4:19–21; 8:24–26; 14:25)
- heals the sick (Mark 1:32–34; 8:23–25; Luke 17:12–14)
- raises the dead (Mark 5:35–36, 40–42; Luke 7:12–15; John 11:43–44)
- is a prophet (Matt. 16:13–14; Luke 24:19)
- existed before all creation (John 1:3)
- is the Word of God (John 1:1, 14; Heb. 4:12)
- is the Lamb of God (John 1:36)
- is the way, the truth, and the life (John 14:6)
- rose from the dead (John 20:26–28)
- ascended to heaven (Acts 1:9)
- is now alive with God in heaven (Mark 16:19)
- will return (Acts 1:11)
- will have an unmistakable second coming (Matt. 24:26–27)
- intercedes for humanity (Rom. 8:34)
- will judge the living and the dead (Acts 10:42; Heb. 7:25)
- has always existed (John 8:58)
- is the resurrection and the life (John 11:25–26)

Read Bible verses like these and explain that Jesus is more than a prophet. Trust me, this is a crucial point for Muslim listeners. Emphasize the titles of Jesus in Scripture to move the conversation toward the redemption of Christ. Keep focused on his identity as the Messiah, the Son of God, and the Word of

God. Focus on a few names of the Savior in each conversation. Here we'll look at several of them.

JESUS AS THE SON OF GOD

When the sun rises, the stars disappear. As Muslims see the true brilliance of God's Son, the weaker lights in their lives will vanish. Spend as much of your time as possible talking about Jesus's names and miracles, and the light of the good news will begin to dawn on your Muslim friends.

For example, Muslims say they believe in one God. One of the names for Allah is *al-Wahid*. This means "the One" or "the only one." To them, Christ can't be the Word of God incarnate because Allah is "the only one." Al-Wahid as a name of Allah is mentioned in Qur'an 12:39, 14:48, and 38:65.

However, the Arabic word describes *oneness*, not singleness. We Christians also accept that God is one—one God existing eternally in three persons. This truth provides a good beginning for our conversations. As we saw in an earlier chapter, God is *one*—not a lonely, single being—ever existent with his Word and his Spirit.

JESUS AS THE INCARNATE WORD OF GOD

Al-Waheed, another Arabic name for Allah, turns out to be a good Arabic name specifically for our Savior Jesus. He *is the one and only incarnate Word of God*. To be incarnate is to be embodied in flesh or human form. The Word became flesh, a union demonstrating that Jesus is Al-Waheed, the one and only, the Son of God. As John 1:14 says, "The Word became flesh and made his dwelling among us. We have seen his glory, the glory of the one and only Son, who came from the Father, full of grace and truth."

In this same vein, Jesus is also called *Immanuel* (Isa. 7:14; Matt. 1:23), which is a Hebrew word meaning "God is with us." Jesus is God's Word given in physical form. Jesus is the incarnation of the Almighty God; he submitted to death on a cross because it was God's will and because it would glorify God. In doing so, he proved to be stronger than sin and death, and proved his right to the name Jesus *Christ*: Jesus the *Messiah*.

In Islam, did you know that Muslims are taught that the Qur'an is the eternal word of God, existing with God from eternity to eternity? That word of God, Muslims are told, was dictated to Muhammad verse by verse, through the revelation of the angel Gabriel, and is both temporal and eternal. Imam al-Ghazali (ca. 1056–1111) explained that God and his word are of the same essence, therefore, God and his word are one—and Islam is a monotheistic religion.

God's oneness with his word is great background as you speak with a Muslim. Are God and his word the same or different? Because of al-Ghazali, all Muslims will say they are the same. This leads to an obvious point: if Jesus is the Word of God, then he is equal with God. Jesus is the incarnation of the Word of God, so he is temporal and eternal at the same time. Muslims should understand this concept as you explain who Jesus is.

To sum up, Jesus is one with the Almighty One (al-Wahid) and he is the one and only incarnation of God (al-Waheed). Jesus is the Son of the living God. Let your Muslim friends in on this good news!

55 Seconds for Change

Muslims are aware of Judgment Day—*very* aware. Islam teaches that when Muslims die, they experience the torture of the grave by two angels. Muslim fear of the grave is real. Added to that, Muslims can't fully trust Allah, since he can change his mind on a whim and send a righteous person into hellfire.

The refreshing message of the gospel could not stand in greater contrast. We proclaim that God is holy and faithful. He saves us and welcomes us, not for our righteousness but according to the righteousness of Jesus, who is the one and only incarnate Word of God. As such, he can be trusted to care for us and meet our deepest needs—even on Judgment Day. In the place of torture, followers of Jesus can expect pure love and grace. Judgment Day is therefore a time of celebration, not fear, for those who are ready.

Pray for a Muslim friend or acquaintance, asking for an opportunity to share the gospel of forgiveness and grace with him or her.

Chapter 18

THE PAUL MYTH

I was leading a seminar on reaching Muslims for Christ at a church in Indianapolis. An older math professor from Pakistan and three young engineers were in the audience. They were all Muslims, curious to hear what I was teaching. During the afternoon break, one of the engineers walked to the front and placed a Bible on the table in front of me—one with the words of Jesus printed in red letters. He said, "I believe in what I find in red, and nothing else. For example, I reject the teachings of Paul."

I smiled and said, "Great! If you follow the red letters, then you're a Christian."

A statement like this will confuse the Muslims, who believe Paul invented Christianity. That's right—like some skeptical scholars of religion, some Muslims think that the apostle Paul influenced people to believe that Jesus was the Son of God, when really he was only a human prophet. The apostle Paul is a major leader in the early church, and his letters to early followers of Christ are incorporated in the New Testament. Some Islamic teachers have presented the idea that Paul, not the Messiah Jesus, created the teachings of Christianity.

So if a Muslim says they believe only the red letters—the

quotes of Jesus—you can offer to have a Bible study on Jesus's statements. As we saw in the previous chapter, they're life-changing!

However, your Muslim friend needs to see that Paul's writings and the rest of the New Testament agree with what Jesus taught about himself. The following points can help you expose the myth that Paul invented Christianity and aid Muslims in moving from this fallacy to facts, and from facts to faith.

CHRISTIAN CHURCHES EXISTED BEFORE PAUL

Paul wasn't the first disciple of Jesus. When he became a Christian in Damascus, the Christian community already existed (Acts 9). This community was made up of those who followed Jesus and saw his crucifixion and resurrection. Obviously, Paul couldn't have invented a faith that already existed.

AT FIRST, PAUL HATED CHRISTIANS

The Christian community was multiplying, and Paul, who was a Pharisee, supported killing the followers of Jesus (Acts 7:55–58; 9:1–2). Why then would he join this community and bolster their faith in Jesus?

PAUL EXPERIENCED A RADICAL CONVERSION

When Saul became a Christian and was baptized, he used a different name to show the change in his life—Paul. One of the leaders in the early church, Barnabas, took care of him and brought him to the Christian community.

> When he came to Jerusalem, he tried to join the disciples, but they were all afraid of him, not believing that he really was a disciple. But Barnabas took him and brought him to the apostles. He told them how Saul on his journey had seen the Lord and that the Lord had spoken to him, and how in Damascus he had preached fearlessly in the name of Jesus. So Saul stayed with them and moved about freely in Jerusalem, speaking boldly in the name of the Lord. (Acts 9:26–28)

The Christian community in Jerusalem was afraid of Saul because they knew that as a Pharisee, he'd been killing Jesus's followers. The church in Jerusalem knew Stephen and others whom Saul had killed. Therefore, it took a Christian leader to protect the converted Paul and introduce him to the Christian community.

THE NAME *CHRISTIAN* WAS GIVEN TO THE COMMUNITY

Paul couldn't have invented Christianity, because he himself was trained by the Christian community—in Jerusalem, in Arabia, and in Antioch. In Antioch, the Christians were called that name by the pagans around them because this new community talked about and obeyed the teachings of Jesus the Christ. The English word *Christ* is the translation for the Greek word *christos*, which means "anointed one," which in turn is a translation of the Hebrew term *mashiach*, which we translate in English as

"Messiah." The believers talked about Christ so often that they became known as Christians.

This name wasn't "invented" by someone. It wasn't given to a class or a club that Paul started; it grew among a whole community.

In Acts, we see Paul being discipled in the Christian community of Antioch: "Barnabas went to Tarsus to look for Saul, and when he found him, he brought him to Antioch. So for a whole year Barnabas and Saul met with the church and taught great numbers of people. The disciples were called Christians first at Antioch" (Acts 11:25–26).

PAUL GAVE HIS LIFE FOR
THIS MESSAGE

Paul details, in one of his letters from prison (2 Cor. 11:23–28), all his many sufferings to spread the message of Jesus. Eventually he would die in Rome for spreading the Christian faith. Why would Paul do all this if he didn't believe in a risen Jesus? Why would he write all those letters to encourage others if he didn't believe what he was writing and if he could be executed for preaching about Jesus?

PAUL WROTE MUCH OF THE
NEW TESTAMENT

Paul began ministering and sharing the gospel after his conversion and baptism in Damascus. Many of the Jewish leaders tried to stop him, and with Rome's help, they ended up imprisoning him. As a Roman citizen, Paul appealed to Caesar, meaning he would be chained and taken from his homeland to Rome, the capital of the Roman Empire, for a hearing.

Overall, Paul wrote thirteen of the New Testament's twenty-seven "books." Four of them are known as his "prison epistles"—Ephesians, Philippians, Colossians, and Philemon—each named for its recipients. Paul's letters were encouragements, teachings, and expositions of Jesus's message. These epistles were written earlier than the gospels of Matthew, Mark, Luke, and John. Why is this important? Paul's writings were accessible for critique by other Christian leaders. If Paul had "invented" something, wouldn't these leaders have put a stop to it in their ministry and writings?

PAUL FOUGHT WITH BARNABAS

Muslim leaders often claim that Paul's fight with Barnabas described in Acts proves that the heretical Gospel of Barnabas is correct. This document, which bears evidence of having been written hundreds of years after Barnabas lived, claims, like Islam, that Jesus was spared the cross. Paul corrupted the true gospel, they say; that's why the Gospel of Barnabas was lost. Even today, this false gospel is distributed in Muslim countries and propagated on the internet. It is a fake, filled with anachronisms.

In the book of Acts, we instead see that Paul and Barnabas fought over ministry and team structure, not theology. Paul was a disciple of Barnabas, and the fight concerned whether Mark, a young follower of Jesus, should be invited on their mission trip (Acts 15:36–41).

Paul and Barnabas's conflict led ultimately to a positive outcome. We see how, through this dispute, God used both Paul and Barnabas and had two trips to bless rather than one. Barnabas was the ever-encouraging friend who led many to grow in their faith; Paul was the fiery evangelist and apologist with the determination and spirit to spread the gospel in the most difficult places. Christ changed their lives and used the gifts of both men toward different goals, but neither invented nor changed Christianity.

55 Seconds for Change

Read the following autobiography of Paul, and ask Jesus to similarly transform someone you know into his devoted follower.

> If anyone else thinks he has reason for confidence in the flesh, I have more: circumcised on the eighth day, of the people of Israel, of the tribe of Benjamin, a Hebrew of Hebrews; as to the law, a Pharisee; as to zeal, a persecutor of the church; as to righteousness under the law, blameless. But whatever gain I had, I counted as loss for the sake of Christ . . . because of the surpassing worth of knowing Christ Jesus my Lord. For his sake I have suffered the loss of all things and count them as rubbish, in order that I may gain Christ and be found in him, not having a righteousness of my own that comes from the law, but that which comes through faith in Christ, the righteousness from God that depends on faith—that I may know him and the power of his resurrection, and may share his sufferings, becoming like him in his death, that by any means possible I may attain the resurrection from the dead.
>
> Not that I have already obtained this or am already perfect, but I press on to make it my own, because Christ Jesus has made me his own. Brothers, I do not consider that I have made it my own. But one thing I do: forgetting what lies behind and straining forward to what lies ahead, I press on toward the goal for the prize of the upward call of God in Christ Jesus. (Phil. 3:4-14 ESV)

Chapter 19

CORRUPTION OF
THE BIBLE

I once led eleven Americans on a trip to Beirut. While we were there, we went downtown to enjoy some of the city's famous baklava. As we entered a store, the owner asked me if I was a Christian. I answered that, yes, all of us were; we were in the city to pray that God would bless Beirut.

The storeowner said, "Christians are wrong. They follow the Injeel, and the Injeel has been corrupted."

"God forbid!" I exclaimed. "If all the Christians got together and tried to change the Injeel, who would win, God or the Christians?"

He was taken aback and asked me to repeat my question, so I did.

"Of course," he replied, "God would win."

"You're right," I replied. "This means that no one can change the Injeel. No one is stronger than God, and it's a blasphemy to say that humans can corrupt God's Word."

The shopkeeper's demeanor changed, and so did his defensive attitude. "I've never heard anything like this," he confessed.

Muslims are taught that the Bible has been corrupted. If we are to make headway in sharing the good news with them, we must be able to answer this charge. Again, apologetics are a must. But don't worry—we have answers that we (and they) can trust. The ability to show these truths will provide a foundation for sharing the gospel with our Muslim friends.

An important point in our favor is that Muslims are taught at a fundamental level to respect the four holy books: the Torah (al-Tawrat), the Psalms (Az-Zabur), the New Testament (al-Injeel), and the Qur'an. But because the prevailing belief in the Islamic world is that the Bible cannot be trusted, Muslims need an *ambassador* for God's Word, a compassionate guide to show them the depth, beauty, and integrity of the Bible. They need and deserve an authentic Christian friend who can share with them the life-transforming truth of Scripture.[12] They need *you*!

WHAT DOES THE QUR'AN SAY ABOUT THE INJEEL?

As we've seen, *Injeel* is the Arabic word used for the New Testament. So what does the Qur'an say about the Injeel?

- Al-Injeel is sent from God.
  Allah! There is no god worthy of worship except Him— the Ever-Living, All-Sustaining. He has revealed to you O Prophet the Book in truth, confirming what came before it, as He revealed the Torah and the Gospel. (Qur'an 3:2–3)

- Muslims must read and believe in the Injeel.

  Say, O believers, "We believe in Allah and what has been revealed to us; and what was revealed to Abraham, Ishmael, Isaac, Jacob, and his descendants; and what was given to Moses, Jesus, and other prophets from their Lord. We make no distinction between any of them. And to Allah we all submit." (Qur'an 2:136)

  Then in the footsteps of these prophets, We sent Our messengers, and after them We sent Jesus, son of Mary, and granted him the Gospel, and instilled compassion and mercy into the hearts of his followers. As for monasticism, they made it up—We never ordained it for them—only seeking to please Allah, yet they did not even observe it strictly. So We rewarded those of them who were faithful. But most of them are rebellious. (Qur'an 57:27)

- Christians are friends to Muslims.

  You will surely find the most bitter towards the believers to be the Jews and polytheists and the most gracious to be those who call themselves Christian. That is because there are priests and monks among them and because they are not arrogant. (Qur'an 5:82)

- Christians must judge all revelation by the Injeel.

  So let the people of the Gospel judge by what Allah has revealed in it. And those who do not judge by what Allah has revealed are truly the rebellious. (Qur'an 5:47)

  Say, O Prophet, "O People of the Book! You have nothing to stand on unless you observe the Torah, the

Gospel, and what has been revealed to you from your Lord." And your Lord's revelation to you O Prophet will only cause many of them to increase in wickedness and disbelief. So do not grieve for the people who disbelieve." (Qur'an 5:68)

- God keeps his word.
  Surely Allah is Most Capable of everything. (Qur'an 2:148)

Many imams teach what is contrary to the previous qur'anic verses. They uphold that only the Qur'an, among God's books, is uncorrupted, yet the Qur'an itself never makes such a claim!

WHAT DOES THE INJEEL SAY ABOUT ITSELF?

Muslims would be wise to pay attention to the awesome claims the New Testament makes about itself. They include the following: God inspired all Scripture (2 Tim. 3:16–17; 2 Peter 1:20–21), God's Word stands firm and will be fulfilled (Matt. 5:17–18; 24:35), the Word of God endures and brings life (Mark 13:31; 1 Peter 1:23), and God protects his Word (Rev. 22:18–19).

The Injeel insists that God protects his Word. The Zabur (Psalms) and Tawrat (Torah, or Pentateuch) make this claim as well.

From the Tawrat:

"As for me, this is my covenant with them," says the LORD: "My Spirit who is on you, and my words that I have put

in your mouth, will not depart from your mouth, or from
the mouths of your children, or from the mouths of your
children's children, from now on and forever," says the LORD.
(Isa. 59:21 CSB)

From the Zabur:

> LORD, your word is forever;
> it is firmly fixed in heaven. (Ps. 119:89 CSB)

Once we get past barriers of misunderstanding and misper-
ception, Christians and Muslims can have wonderful conversations about God's messages to humanity. Both faiths believe
that God sent the Tawrat of Moses, the Zabur of David, and
the Injeel of Jesus. Even though many imams say that these
first three messages were corrupted, when you invite a Muslim
to read the Bible, you are encouraging them to be obedient to
their chosen faith—because the Qur'an commands its followers
to read them, along with the Qur'an.

ESTABLISHING THE
AUTHENTICITY OF THE INJEEL

Since your Muslim friends have grown up in a completely different belief system, they may need time to process a new way
of thinking about the Injeel. Eventually they will also have to
carefully weigh the personal cost of accepting the Injeel and its
teachings about Jesus.

The rest of this chapter lays out different approaches, or
directions, from which you can build a loving, gentle, and

patient bridge from where your friend is now to confidence that the Injeel is God's pure and uncorrupted message to all of us.

Keep in mind that Muslims commonly believe that God sent the Tawrat to Moses but that the Jewish people changed it; God sent the Zabur to David, but the Jews changed that also; and God sent the Injeel to Christians, but the Christians changed it to suit their own desires. God finally sent the Qur'an, which is incorruptible.

The imams teach that we Christians have made many changes to the New Testament over time, creating a series of different versions, so that the original meaning has been lost. They believe Jesus originally taught about the prophet to come, Muhammad, and the "true" faith of Islam but that we have changed many of the stories and have deleted all references to Muhammad and to Islam. Therefore, they say, our present Bible isn't true to the words of Jesus; it's unreliable, corrupted with human teachings.

The Biblical Foundation

We believe what the Bible says about itself. For example, 2 Timothy 3:16 says that the Injeel is the inspired, or "God-breathed," Word of God. That is, God himself moved upon the writers and caused them to write accurately about the words and actions of Jesus, as well as the lives of those in the rest of the Bible. Christians believe that God sent his Word—the Old and New Testaments of our Bible.

We also believe that God himself protects and preserves his Word because he is omnipotent. He does this to enlighten and to judge humanity. He gives light as an act of gracious love. And if he is to be a just judge, he must preserve his Word accurately so that we can be held accountable to it.

What about the "many versions" of the Bible that your Muslim friend may have heard about? All those "translations"? They are merely varied wordings of the same ancient manuscripts. The basis of the Bible is unchanged; but as languages change over time, we adapt our translations to be understood in our day. For many years, people in the West used the King James Version, which was originally translated in 1611. But some of its wording, such as translating the word for *love* as "charity," is now archaic. But the King James and the newer translations are taken mostly from the same ancient Bible manuscripts, although the newer translations reflect better, even more accurate scholarship than in the past.

Your Approach When Discussing the Injeel

Whenever Muslims ask about our Scriptures' reliability or state that the Bible is corrupted, you can respond on three levels: *theological*, *logical*, and *historical*. This material is presented in more depth in my book *Connecting with Muslims: A Guide to Communicating Effectively*. I commend that book to you and summarize the main points here for our current discussion.

Theological Reasoning

Always start with the theological. Let's say you're sitting together over a cup of tea, and your friend says, "Well, the Injeel has been corrupted."

When Muslims say this or something like it, you might respond as I did in an earlier anecdote. I said, *"Astaghfirullah!"* This Arabic expression means "God forbid" or "God forgive you for blasphemy."

In a Muslim community, regardless of culture, it is imperative not to insult God. The name of God, "Allah," is frequently invoked into the language of the community. It can be used in greetings and blessings and to ward off curses or calamities.

When you as a follower of Christ reveal your honor to God by not offending his power and wisdom, your Muslim friend will be compelled to listen. This theological part of the conversation is aimed at helping Muslims respect God by reading the Injeel.

Next, read or recite an appropriate verse from the Bible, which is the Word of God and is able to answer for itself. I recommend Mark 13:31: "Heaven and earth will pass away, but my words will never pass away."

Explain to your friend that if God sent the Injeel, God will protect it. No one is stronger than God, and no one can change his message if he chooses to keep it unchanged. Qur'an 2:148 is a beautiful verse that says, in essence, "God can do all things," and in this it agrees with our Bible. (For example, see Gen. 18:14; Luke 1:37; 18:27.)

Logical Reasoning

Simple logic is also tremendously useful. If your friend claims that the Injeel has been corrupted, consider asking the following questions.

- *Who* changed the Injeel? Many will answer that the apostle Paul was the primary culprit or that Christians made the changes.
- So *why* would somebody want to change the Injeel? The most common response is that the changes were motivated by the Christians' unwillingness to follow the true God, Allah, or his prophet, Muhammad.

- *Where* was the Injeel corrupted? This answer may vary, but many believe that Paul or other Christians made the changes at Rome.
- *Where* is the original Injeel? How do they know it's been changed, unless they know where the original is? An accusation without evidence is unconvincing.
- *What* parts of the Injeel are corrupted? The standard answer is that Christians changed many stories and deleted all mentions of Islam and Muhammad. Again, there is no research to back up this claim.
- *When* was the Injeel corrupted? Was it before or after the life of Muhammad? Some claim that Paul changed the Injeel in AD 325. But since Paul died around AD 63–64—more than 260 years earlier—this is impossible.

Muhammad, on the other hand, lived from AD 570–632, and he announced that he was a prophet in 610. If the Injeel had been corrupted before Muhammad's time, then Christians would have been following a corrupt book for hundreds of years, and Muhammad would have warned his followers about this corruption. But the Qur'an states clearly that it came to *confirm*—not to replace or correct—the message of Jesus and that Muhammad instructed his followers to believe in the Tawrat of Moses, the Zabur of David, and the Injeel of Jesus (Qur'an 3:2–3; 4:163; 17:55; 9:111).

Not once does the Qur'an say that any parts of our Bible have been changed. That assertion was added later as Islam conquered Christian-majority nations. When you invite Muslims to read the Bible, you're simply asking them to obey the teaching of the Qur'an and to follow the teachings of Jesus.

Historical Reasoning

Here's a simple way to demonstrate that the Injeel has not been changed. Start by drawing a long horizontal line, then divide it into three segments.

1. Eyewitnesses stage
2. Persecution stage
3. Translation stage

Explain these three time periods to your Muslim friend. Segment 1, the eyewitness stage (AD 1–100), is the period during which the eyewitnesses of Jesus's life, miracles, teachings, crucifixion, and resurrection were alive. During this time the Injeel couldn't have been changed because those who knew the truth firsthand would have stood up and confronted the lie.

But what if the eyewitnesses were the liars? That question might arise. What if *they* were the ones who changed the Injeel? Hundreds of eyewitnesses of Jesus's life were martyred for their Christian faith, including the apostles and later the apostle Paul himself. If these men had changed the Injeel, would they have been willing to die for their own lie?

By AD 100 the eyewitnesses of Jesus's life were all gone. This begins segment 2, the persecution stage, which lasted from AD 100–325. Christians were persecuted throughout this period. Throughout the Mediterranean world, we have found thousands of manuscripts from this period. While not one of them contains the entire New Testament, together they easily construct the full New Testament.

The generations of church leaders who continued on after the original disciples had died wrote numerous letters, sermons, and other documents that included Bible quotations. If the

Injeel had been changed during this period, we would expect numerous contradictions among the thousands of documents, reflecting the older and newer (changed) versions. But other than some insignificant grammatical variations, all these documents agree with one another. Our conclusion: the Injeel was not changed during this time period.

Now, in segment 3, the translation stage (fourth century–present), complete copies of the Greek New Testament show up. The oldest copy of the entire New Testament is Codex Sinaiticus, which dates to the middle of the fourth century. In the manuscripts in this period, we find once again that there are no significant changes.

What about present-day translations? These are all translated directly from the Greek manuscripts, the most reliable of which are dated between AD 100 and 400. Today's translations contain exactly the same message and meaning as in the Greek manuscripts—just in a different language. The Injeel of fourth century is the same as the Injeel of today.

Interestingly, in all three historical stages, from Jesus to today, we find the verse in the Injeel where Jesus said, "I am the way and the truth and the life" (John 14:6)—among hundreds of other uniquely Christian truth claims. If Jesus had said, "Muhammad is coming after me," or "I'm only one of many ways," someone would have written it down during the eyewitness stage. Then it would have shown up in the manuscripts of the persecution stage and the translation stage, and it would be in our Bibles today.

The point is, the message that Jesus taught is the same as the message of our New Testament translations today—corruption-free.

BE PATIENT, NOT PUSHY

After understanding all this, your friend might be eager to read the Injeel and respect it as God's message. This is tremendous progress, but remember, we're building a bridge. And that bridge isn't yet complete. Your friend may have had a change of mind, but has he or she experienced a change of will? The bridge is complete only when he or she has reached the point of decision.

But be patient, not pushy. These insights about the Injeel is new information to them, and your friend may be considering a radical change in his or her entire view of reality and eternity. He or she is likely to say something like, "I'm sorry, this is all new for me."

Accept this reluctance graciously; it's normal. But offer your friend a copy of the Injeel. Most Muslims, after they've heard the theological, logical, and historical reasoning above, will gladly accept one. Your friend might even want to study the Bible with you. So ask!

But remember: don't overstay your welcome in any one conversation. Just keep building your friendship, trusting God to open your friend's heart.

55 Seconds for Change

Take a blank piece of paper. On one side, list the three ways to demonstrate the accuracy and integrity of the Bible, filling in as many details as you can recall from this chapter. On the other side, list the three segments of history, and tell briefly why they assure us that the Bible we have today is substantially the same as in the days of the apostles. Then check your answers.

Chapter 20

THE FICKLE GOD

In current debates about whether Islam is a religion of peace or a religion of violence, much hinges on the Muslim doctrine of abrogation. On the one side are those who quote Qur'an 2:256, which says, "Let there be no compulsion in religion." On the other are those who cite Qur'an 9:5, which says, "But once the Sacred Months have passed, kill the polytheists who violated their treaties wherever you find them, capture them, besiege them, and lie in wait for them." Which do we choose?

Many Muslims today will say the latter, as the doctrine of abrogation has come to the fore. Briefly, we can define it as a belief that certain teachings of the Qur'an have been repealed and replaced—abrogated—by later qur'anic revelations. Abrogation, in essence, allows for the Qur'an to supersede itself in places and for later revelation to overturn earlier revelation. In this case, 9:5 came later, during Islam's warlike phase at the end of Muhammad's life, than 2:256, which was given when Islam was in a position of weakness. Many contemporary Muslim scholars, though not all, believe this.

The doctrine has support in the Muslim holy book. As the Qur'an says, "When We replace a verse with another—and

Allah knows best what He reveals—they say, 'You Muḥammad are just a fabricator.' In fact, most of them do not know." (Qur'an 16:101).

Many Muslims also believe that the Qur'an, which came later in history than the Hebrew Bible and the New Testament, can abrogate these earlier revelations from God.

So as we share Christ with our Muslim friends, many will have this teaching of abrogation in the backs of their minds. This will make them predisposed to think that Islam's religious rituals and doctrines are better than ours. Some may even take abrogation to mean that Muhammad was perfect and infallible, though Islam teaches that he was just a man.

The doctrine of abrogation has several weaknesses. This chapter will give you some ideas on how to use conversational apologetics to reveal them while gently moving the conversation to the uniqueness of Jesus.

ABROGATION ATTACKS THE WISDOM OF GOD

Help your Muslim friend to see that God's revelations must be consistent or else his wisdom must be questioned. Muslims and Christians agree wholeheartedly that God, the creator of heaven and earth, is wise beyond all human understanding. Yet abrogation suggests that God *isn't* all that wise, for he will change his teachings from year to year and generation to generation. Why would God change his mind if he is the fountain of all wisdom? Wouldn't he get it right the first time?

Muslims might counter that we see something similar

happening with the Bible, with the New Testament replacing the Old Testament. But this isn't true; the New Testament came to *fulfill* the Old Testament. As Jesus said, "Do not think that I have come to abolish the Law or the Prophets; I have not come to abolish them but to fulfill them" (Matt. 5:17). Compare the Ten Commandments and the Sermon on the Mount with your Muslim friend. Many followers of Islam are surprised when they see how the Sermon on the Mount (Matthew 5–7) is *built* on the earlier revelation and adds new understanding about God's expectations, particularly as it focuses on the spiritual requirements of the Law. For as our Lord also said, "You have heard that it was said to those of old, 'You shall not murder; and whoever murders will be liable to judgment.' But I say to you that everyone who is angry with his brother will be liable to judgment; whoever insults his brother will be liable to the council; and whoever says, 'You fool!' will be liable to the hell of fire" (Matt. 5:21–22 ESV).

God's revelations are consistent as they expand in scope. If abrogation is true, then the wisdom seen in God's progressive revelation disappears. Instead of a fuller understanding of the truth, we are faced with one contradiction after another, both within the Qur'an and between the holy books of Islam and Christianity.

Consider 2 Peter 3:9, which says, "The Lord is not slow in keeping his promise, as some understand slowness. Instead he is patient with you, not wanting anyone to perish, but everyone to come to repentance." What a beautiful description of our patient and loving God! Yet Muslims might say God abrogated this older command in the New Testament with a new command in the Qur'an:

So when you meet the disbelievers in battle, strike their necks until you have thoroughly subdued them, then bind them firmly. Later free them either as an act of grace or by ransom until the war comes to an end. So will it be. Had Allah willed, He Himself could have inflicted punishment on them. But He does this only to test some of you by means of others. And those who are martyred in the cause of Allah, He will never render their deeds void. (Qur'an 47:4)

This is a stark contradiction. Which is it: patience or beheadings? Love your enemies, or kill them? And if we say beheadings are now God's will in dealing with people of other faiths, how is this different from the Romans, the Persians, and African kingdoms that practiced beheading their enemies? Is this what God really wants?

ABROGATION AND THE LIFE OF MUHAMMAD

Anywhere you go in the Muslim world, Muslim scholars will uphold the life of Muhammad in Arabia as the model for all people in all cultures in all generations. Most Muslims will do the same. Interestingly, many of Islam's abrogated verses and teachings are directly related to his life.

For example, polygamy replaced monogamy, which the Qur'an had endorsed, because the prophet of Islam practiced it. In another example of what we can only call the retrograde cultural power of Islam, the taking of child brides, once taboo, became legal. Why? The prophet of Islam had married a six-year-old girl named Aisha.

Furthermore, Islam says that God also gave Muhammad permission to marry Zainab bint Jahsh, his daughter-in-law by Zaid, his adopted son. This action abrogated earlier qur'anic verses and cultural traditions by revealing to the prophet a new qur'anic verse. Then, after the wedding, Allah supposedly abrogated the teaching of adoption, thus making Zaid no longer the adopted son of Muhammad and clearing any further objections against the marriage.

Such examples of abrogation naturally raise questions: Why would God want to abrogate adoption, which can help orphans? Why would God abrogate adoption *after* Muhammad married Zainab? Such questions will help your Muslim friend begin to see how the whole idea of abrogation demeans God's greatness and wisdom.

ABROGATION ATTACKS
THE POWER OF GOD

In response to these troubling facts, some Muslims simply claim that God abrogates his messages after people corrupt them. But this argument is far from satisfactory. If this were true, wouldn't God's sovereignty and power be undermined? How could God Almighty's teachings become corrupted by mere humans? Shouldn't Allah be able to protect and keep his messages intact? We don't deny that people can twist or forget the truth of God. But God always preserves and stands by his revealed message—nothing is ever lost. As Jesus said, "Heaven and earth will pass away, but my words will never pass away" (Matt. 24:35).

In contrast, consider that, according to some Muslim

scholars, women may be stoned or beheaded in Islam. It didn't used to be this way. This change supposedly happened because a teaching in the Hadith (authoritative traditions concerning the life of Muhammad) abrogated a previous qur'anic verse against stoning. Imams claim that this verse was lost. They quote Aisha, who said, "The verse[s] of stoning and of suckling an adult ten times were revealed, and they were (written) on a paper and kept under my bed. When the messenger of Allah expired and we were preoccupied with his death, a goat entered and ate away the paper."[13] What? God Almighty couldn't stop a goat from eating a piece of paper? God couldn't reveal the verse again in another chapter of the Qur'an? God, being all-powerful, permitted this to happen? And for what reason, exactly? If the goat ate the verse, maybe it wasn't important in the first place? Such questions may be helpful to your friend as he or she reconsiders the logic behind the teaching of abrogation.

55 Seconds for Change

The Bible knows nothing about abrogation—the replacement of older verses and revelation with newer verses and revelation. It does, however, speak of *progressive revelation*, where God builds on earlier truth with fresh insight, often for a wider audience. Thus, in Genesis 15, God tells childless Abram that he will bless the world through descendants as numerous as the stars—and the patriarch believes: "Abram believed the Lord, and he credited it to him as righteousness" (Gen. 15:6). Later the apostle Paul cites this as an example of believing and saving faith. As Paul said in Romans 4:13 (ESV), "The promise to Abraham and his offspring that he would be heir of the world did not come through the law but through the righteousness of faith." The promise to Abram is not abrogated; it is fulfilled in the coming of Christ.

Here is a definition of this concept from Ligonier Ministries to think about and absorb: "Progressive revelation means that while Scripture's application to old covenant believers is different in some ways from its application to new covenant believers, we do not reject any of God's Word. It reveals one message of salvation that we cannot fully grasp unless we consider the whole of the Bible."[14]

Jot down three more examples of progressive revelation from Scripture.

Chapter 21

THE "PRACTICAL NATURE" OF ISLAM

On a sunny afternoon in Fremont, California, I sat at a table with leaders from a nearby church community and a neighboring Islamic center. While we were all enjoying the meal and conversation around the table, an imam, an Afghan immigrant, claimed that Islam is the most practical and fair religion. It's fair toward Christians and also toward male-female relationships.

It has been common in the last few decades to hear Muslims claim that *sharia* (Muslim religious law) is the most practical and just system of law. Qur'an 2:187 discusses an Arabic word, *al-hudood*, which means "guidelines" or "boundaries set by God." Many Muslims claim that the practical nature of Islam proves God sent it. These "boundaries" are practical in daily life, they say with utter confidence. Are they?

Before we answer that question, let's explore where sharia laws come from.

The first source is the Qur'an, which is a compilation of 114 *surahs* (chapters) of statements, called *ayat* (verses), recited by Muhammad. The second source is the Hadith. The word *hadith* means "talk," and it refers to a collection of stories on the life of Muhammad and the early Muslim community. Scholars assembled these collections of stories centuries later, after the life of Muhammad.

It's important to note that the stories written about Muhammad in the Hadith can't be verified from a historical perspective. Muslim imams and scholars believe that all these stories happened as presented, yet they all come from Islamic sources; there are no independent sources on the life of Muhammad.

Also, sharia is divided into the two main branches of Islam: Sunni and Shia. And there is no single book or document called sharia law; it's simply a compilation of teachings by Muslim leaders based on religious sources and documents.

Imams used Arabic words such as *qiyas, isnad,* and *ijma* to describe their systems for verifying these stories and issuing their rulings based on them. They also compare legal cases in Islamic history, the life of Muhammad from the Hadith, and the teachings of the Qur'an to issue religious and legal decisions called *fatwas*.

Unfortunately, religious decisions for millions of people— how Muslims may eat, dress, and marry—have been made by a few fallible imams. Even as they continue to insist that sharia is fair, advocates sidestep problematic issues in Islamic history and the social disasters evident in many Muslim countries today. Muslim countries consistently rank low on international measures of human rights and religious freedom. Those not awash in petrodollars must often grapple with low standards of living. Is this practical or fair? Given claims that sharia is a perfect religious, moral, social, and economic system, such questions must be asked. Love demands that we question and attempt to verify such claims.

What follows are a few issues in Islamic law and the supposed "practical nature of Islam" that we can share with our Muslim friends to ultimately point them to the uniqueness and power of the Savior Jesus.

CHILD BRIDES

While traveling to Europe, I had a connecting flight at the Detroit airport. As I waited, I saw an Arab family getting ready to board. I noticed that their seven-year-old daughter wore a hijab. This Islamic apparel denotes that a woman is chaste and pure. I was surprised, since a seven-year-old is just a girl and not eligible for marriage in the United States. But sharia allows the marrying of girls because of the marriage of Aisha to the prophet.

Consequently, for the last 1,400 years, children have been offered as brides to men across the Muslim world. Child brides are still acceptable in many countries. Many Muslims believe that God permits men of all ages to marry girls of all ages.

Aisha, mentioned briefly in the previous chapter, is one of the saddest names in history. She was the daughter of Abu Bakr, a friend of Muhammad and a convert to Islam. All information about Aisha comes from Islamic sources. She was the second wife Muhammad took, after the death of his first wife, Khadija. The Hadith claims that Aisha was married to Muhammad at six years of age, the marriage was consummated at nine, and Muhammad was fifty-three.

Many stories about Islam and Muhammad in the Hadith come from the accounts given by Aisha. Muhammad died when

Aisha was eighteen, and Islamic scholars believe she died forty-seven years later. Islamic teachers claim that her age should not be a point of controversy since child marriages were common in Bedouin societies. They also claim that this story should not be manipulated to justify abuse of young girls.

Even if the marriage to Aisha was acceptable in Bedouin society during the life of Muhammad, how can it be a model of marriage to all men, in all cultures, for all generations? Tragically, when Muslims came to power in the non-Bedouin cultures of Syria, Persia, and North Africa, this practice was forced upon the conquered cultures.

When you're told of the "practical" nature of Islam, respond with questions that help your Muslim friend to look closely at the stories of the Hadith. Ask questions such as:

- Why would Allah allow something like child brides?
- What is the practical nature of taking child brides?
- Would you marry a child or give your daughter as a child bride?

Be clear that this is no criticism of Muhammad, but rather an honest look at the stories in the Hadith and the laws derived from it.

These stories, when discussed sensitively but with a commitment to biblical truth and human dignity, can create a hunger for truth among Muslims. Aisha's stories in the Hadith, whether true or not, depict sadness, anger, and loneliness. Conversely, many Muslim women are eager to know the teachings and example of Jesus concerning women, marriage, and family.

A Syrian refugee family I became aware of had suffered at the hands of ISIS jihadists who wanted their young daughters to be married to older men. But the teachings of Jesus in the Bible were such a fresh blessing to them that the whole family was baptized.

Pray for Muslim women. Pray for women called Aisha. Pray for God to move in these last days and heal the hearts of Muslims.

PEACEFUL RELIGION

Muslims often say Islam is a peaceful religion. And indeed, many Muslims *are* peaceful. They are interested in religious conversations and want their communities to grow and flourish. These are all good things.

However, the teachings of the Qur'an on jihad and warfare inevitably entangle great numbers of Muslims in war and violence, at least tacitly. Let's remember that *peace* in Arabic is the word *salam*, and the related word *Islam* comes from *salama*, which means "to surrender." Yes, Islam is a religion of peace, but unfortunately it is the kind of peace that follows conquests and subjugation.

Islam's teachings on jizya, a religious tax imposed on non-Muslims, go hand in hand with the religion's teachings about war. The Qur'an in verses 9:5, 29, 111 commands war and a religious tax against non-Muslims. ISIS actions against Christians during the battle of Mosul from 2016–2017 were directly inspired by 9:29: "Fight those who do not believe in Allah and the Last Day, nor comply with what Allah and His Messenger have forbidden, nor embrace the religion of truth from among those who were given the Scripture, until they pay the tax, willingly submitting, fully humbled."

When your friend mentions the practical nature of sharia, ask him or her the following questions:

- What do you mean by the statement, "Islam is a peaceful religion"?
- Is Islam peaceful toward other religions?
- What does peace mean to you?
- Have you read the verses on peace in the Bible?

While I was speaking with a Sunni Muslim from the Middle East over a cup of Turkish coffee, the topic of jizya came up in relation to peaceful treatment of the "people of the book" (Jews and Christians) in Muslim nations. I asked him, "How much is jizya?"

He didn't know. I then asked him, "Why should one citizen pay another citizen, just because they are from different religions? Historically, the jizya was used to oppress Christians. I think we need to see exactly what Jesus says about human relationships."

Immediately his ears perked up, and I read from my Bible app, finding the verses where Jesus says to love our neighbors as ourselves (Matt. 22:39) and to love our enemies (Matt. 5:44). My friend was shocked to discover that these are core teachings of Christianity. We take these truths for granted; to Muslims they're a wonderful surprise.

HIJAB

Muslim teachers claim that the piety and chastity of women are of utmost importance in Islam, contrary to other religions. Across the Muslim world, different shapes and forms of the hijab are used, from those covering the hair to those covering the face and body (called a *niqab* or burka).

Islamic teaching stresses that wearing the hijab is a sign of the presence of Islam in a community. It also stresses that Muslim women may choose to wear or not wear the hijab (though sometimes it is mandated) and that the hijab will help men not to lust after women. Islam puts the responsibility for chastity therefore on women, making them carry the shame or the honor of the community.

But the Bible puts the responsibility on men to control their minds, eyes, and behavior. As Jesus said, "I tell you that anyone who looks at a woman lustfully has already committed adultery with her in his heart" (Matt. 5:28). Lust begins in the mind, and the hijab, despite all the claims for its practicality, does not solve the problem of sin.

Good questions to ask about the hijab include:

- Why are you wearing the hijab?
- Is it a social solution or a spiritual solution?
- Do you agree with all the teachings of Islam?
- Are men responsible for their thoughts?
- Have you read what Jesus says about adultery?

A Saudi student in Arizona who was investigating the Bible attended a Bible study for several months. There, touched by the life and teachings of Christ, she received Jesus as her Savior. A few months after her baptism, she decided to take off the hijab.

When this student's pastor asked her why, she replied, "Jesus says anyone who commits sin is a slave of sin, but if the Son sets you free you are free indeed! The hijab I wore is a sign that I was not set free."

55 Seconds for Change

Islam claims to be a practical religion, but Muslim sharia law fails to live up to this promise. It leaves us with child brides, oppression of non-Muslims, and coercion of women. Jesus is different, giving all people dignity. He invites us to be part of his family. He explains to us that he is the vine and we are the branches (John 15:1–8). We are connected to him through love and grace rather than enslaving laws and regulations.

Every time a woman wears the hijab, she is saying she submits to Islam and all its teachings. When you see such women, pray that they would come to the liberating knowledge of the Savior Jesus. Many Muslims yearn for the spiritual freedom found only in Christ. Pray that their spiritual veils are lifted (2 Cor. 3:14).

Ask God to create in you a heart like the prophet Deborah's—a heart for justice and to defend the weak. Pray that you will always speak up for the defense of women and children who are vulnerable because of sharia law.

Abba, Father, you are the God of justice and mercy. You care for the widows and the orphans. Make me an instrument of your will. May I always defend the weak and those who suffer under sharia law. Bless Muslims today and draw them closer to faith in you. In Jesus's name. Amen.

Chapter 22

LEAVING
ISLAM

Following Christ can be costly when you have spent your whole life following Muhammad. Christian conversion means profound change for every part of a person's life. Muslims may face the severe displeasure of friends and family. Those who decide to follow Jesus have their motives questioned. Seeing this kind of backlash, other inquiring Muslims wonder, "Why would I want to leave Islam and incur persecution?" Given these incredible pressures, we must help Muslims understand the urgency of salvation—that knowing Christ and attaining salvation are worth any price.

Such life-changing conversions are happening more often than most people think. As I mentioned earlier, in the last twenty years, more Muslims have come to follow Christ than in the previous centuries.[15] Muslims are responding to him in many ways: after meeting Christians, upon seeing a vision of Jesus, or simply after reading the Bible in their language. I wish you could see the stacks of testimonies I regularly receive in my office.

WHAT KINDS OF MUSLIMS
ARE TURNING TO JESUS?

We are seeing many nominal Muslims come to faith in Christ. In many areas, Islam and culture are entangled, making it difficult for Muslims to decipher which parts of their understanding of Islam are cultural and which are religious.

But many coming to faith are practicing Muslims, not just nominal ones. They know their religion and see the need for a Savior. Some Muslim-background believers wore the hijab for ten or twenty years before getting saved. When you see Muslim men or women become devout in their own faith, keep praying for them. Never give up. That process of becoming devoted and committed to the rituals of Islam can paradoxically draw them closer to faith in Christ. This was the testimony of the apostle Paul, who hated Christianity with religious fervor before embracing it with the same fervor.

REASONS MUSLIMS HESITATE

Many times, as you share with Muslims, they will hesitate about following Christ. Be patient and remember that they're dealing with many hurdles and pressures. Let the Holy Spirit guide you and give you insight and empathy.

Many Muslims believe they're all alone in making such a decision. Islamic teaching asserts that no one leaves Islam. Making this statement plausible in the Muslim world is the continuing reality that Bibles cannot be printed or circulated and that Christian media products are confiscated. Many Muslim countries control the internet and block Christian websites. One Muslim woman thought she was the only one from her country to consider following Jesus, until she went online and found others like her. She ended up meeting others in her country who had decided to follow him. This encouraged her to take the step herself.

Another Sunni woman heard about Muslims becoming followers of Jesus and thought they must not be devout—that maybe they were nominal Muslims just seeking permission to drink alcohol. Not until she read Nabeel Qureshi's book *Seeking Allah, Finding Jesus* did she think differently. She made the same decision for herself because she saw the beautiful character of Christ and the courage of other believers.

A Shia lawyer began his search for the truth by embarking on a comparison between Islam and Christianity. After years of research and study, and seeing the historical evidence pointing toward the truth of the gospel, still he hesitated. Eventually God revealed that family pressure was holding him back. Once he decided that truth was more important than tradition, this lawyer decided to follow Jesus.

Tradition can distract many Muslims from the truth. Many of their traditions are unifying, family-oriented, and fun, such as breaking the fast during the month of Ramadan. While faith in Christ and joining a vibrant Christian community have their own life-affirming traditions—Advent, Easter, and other events, for example—the potential loss of some beloved Muslim traditions must be reckoned with.

So be patient with your Muslim friends and help them see that, in all areas of life, while traditions aren't bad things, they must be tested and compared with the truth of the gospel. Always pray that God will give your friend a sincere heart. God says, "You will seek me and find me when you seek me with all your heart" (Jer. 29:13).

To alleviate their loneliness, let your friends hear from other believers from Muslim backgrounds, in person if possible. If this is not possible, show them videos and testimonies of people who have come to faith in Christ. My ministry's website, crescentproject.org, has many such testimonies that can encourage your Muslim friend.

OVERCOMING BARRIERS
TO THE GOSPEL

Above all, Muslim seekers and believers need to see a *community*. The Muslim faith operates like a community, with all the members watching out for one another. Your Muslim friends need to know there is another community that cares. If they don't see this, they will hesitate. If they feel lonely or secluded, they will hesitate. Jesus commanded us to welcome all people. Jesus commands us to surround our friends and protect them. When Paul faced exclusion from fearful Christians, Barnabas went to him in friendship and shared faith. A cup of cold water will not be forgotten if done in Jesus's name.

The fear your friends face over possibly turning to Jesus as Lord and Savior is very real—and it must be addressed if they are to overcome it. Share Bible verses about God's power over fear. Use chapter 8 of this book to *encourage* the hearts of new or prospective believers.

Finally, use social media wisely. It's imperative that Muslim seekers hear the gospel, not dismissive attacks on Islam. Shine the light of Christ with humility. There is genuine strength in gentleness. All of us prefer dealing with a kind spirit, including Muslims. May God give you wisdom about what social media to use—and how to use it graciously. Let Muslims see the goodness of the gospel, not the bitterness that too often flows into social media posts. Remember, God has sovereignly put you where you are—not to win the argument but to win the person.

We can't afford to let our friendships become tense and aggressive. The truth must be told, and reason must be employed, but rest in the fact that it is God who reveals. God doesn't call us to be prosecuting attorneys but witnesses to the One who loves Muslims. Our part is that of the ambassador; Jesus makes people citizens of the kingdom.

55 Seconds for Change

Matthew 22:37-40 says, "Jesus replied: 'Love the Lord your God with all your heart and with all your soul and with all your mind.' This is the first and greatest commandment. And the second is like it: 'Love your neighbor as yourself.' All the Law and the Prophets hang on these two commandments." These words of the Messiah Jesus speak to us today. Love is what removes these hurdles. Love of God, love for God, and love for our neighbor—this biblical love is unconditional and relational. Pray for a new outlook on your life, neighborhood, and neighbors.

> *God of all creation, you made us and created us. Your glory is seen in this diverse world. Thank you for creating me and redeeming me. My neighbors are created and loved by you, regardless of their religion and behavior. Change my heart and my view. Use my words and actions to show your love to my Muslim neighbors. In Jesus's name. Amen.*

Chapter 23

OUR NEED FOR
A SAVIOR

After I gave a lecture at Wayne State University in Detroit, titled "Jesus in the Qur'an and the Injeel," a man from India approached. Life is a test, he told me, and on Judgment Day our individual, righteous works will be put in a balance. If the good deeds outweigh the bad, a person will attain paradise.

"About Jesus," the Muslim man continued, "it isn't fair for him to pay our debt of sin to God. Each person is responsible for his own sins."

So I asked him, "When do you know you've done enough good works?"

Like many Muslims, he had no answer to this question, so I followed up with another. "If I owed a debt to you, and you forgave me, who has paid my debt to you?"

"I guess it's me. I'm paying your debt for you."

"Exactly, my friend," I replied. "This is what we call redemption in the Christian faith."

Most of the world's religions operate on the fallacy that good works earn salvation. Islam is no exception. We need to help Muslims see the truth of our need for more than good works—we all need a Savior, or we would be doomed by our own wickedness. Christ saves us from the penalty and power of sin. How can we explain this concept to Muslims?

SIN AND SALVATION IN ISLAM

As we've seen, all Muslims believe people will be judged. This teaching from the Qur'an appears to be borrowed from the Bible. Muslims believe that the sovereign Lord of the universe will judge people for every word, attitude, and action. Here are some of the clearest qur'anic verses on the subject:

> O humanity! Be mindful of your Lord, and beware of a Day when no parent will be of any benefit to their child, nor will a child be of any benefit to their parent. (Qur'an 31:33)

> Be mindful of the Day when you will all be returned to Allah, then every soul will be paid in full for what it has done, and none will be wronged. (Qur'an 2:281)

> The weighing on that Day will be just. As for those whose scale will be heavy with good deeds, only they will be successful. (Qur'an 7:8)

Islam also appears to borrow from neighboring Middle Eastern religions in its conception of the afterlife. For example, the road into heaven (called *al-Surat*), the scale on Judgment Day, and the maidens in paradise all are echoed in Egyptian and Persian mythologies. Regardless of how Muslims conceive

Judgment Day, their fear is real. Islam never guarantees that they have performed enough good works.

Dying in jihad (religious warfare), however, is considered the ultimate sacrifice and is the only guarantee of heaven offered in Islam (see Qur'an 9:5 and 9:111). How tragic! The rise in Islamic militancy around the world is thus, at least in part, a sign of a deeper spiritual issue. It shows that Muslim men and women hunger and thirst for assurance of heaven.

This is one reason why gospel proclamation is so urgent. The light of the gospel must pierce such devastating darkness. The same urgency that impelled the disciples forward must also power us as we minister to a world in despair. Jesus's disciples saw God's power in mighty works that emboldened their witness. As the formerly fearful apostle Peter told the members of the Sanhedrin, "This Jesus is the stone that was rejected by you, the builders, which has become the cornerstone. And there is salvation in no one else, for there is no other name under heaven given among men by which we must be saved" (Acts 4:8–12 ESV).

Today the testimonies of Muslims who have found the Savior Jesus will give us similar hope and courage. The gospel is that a Savior was born in Bethlehem, the incarnate Word of God. He died on the cross for our redemption and was raised from the dead on the third day, as the prophets of old said. And he offers the assurance of admission into heaven, which Muslims long for.

CONVERSATIONAL APOLOGETICS

On one occasion, as I sipped coffee with a Muslim friend from Pakistan, the conversation turned to heaven and hell. I asked him how he expected to gain admittance to heaven. "My good works erase my bad works," he replied, "and I will then make it to heaven."

I asked, "What if they're equal—fifty percent good, fifty percent bad?" As I often find, this man, named Muhammad, had no answer. This gave me an opportunity to share the good news that a Savior has come for our rescue.

Here are a couple of ways to respond to your Muslim friends' need for a Savior. First, ask questions that help them realize that righteousness isn't human-based but God-based. *God* decides who is righteous. Ask questions such as these:

- If the scales weighing your good deeds and your bad deeds came out equal, where would you go?
- If a Muslim enters heaven with 90 percent good works, is she on the same level with those who barely make it at 51 percent?
- Does God look at attitudes or actions? Could my actions be different from my attitude?
- Are human efforts righteous enough in the sight of God's holiness?

Second, study the following Bible verses with your Muslim friends, helping them to discover the truth that our works can never be sufficient to open the door of heaven for us. Only faith can do this, by God's grace (unmerited favor).

"The Son of Man came to seek and to save the lost." (Luke 19:10)

It is by grace you have been saved, through faith—and this is not from yourselves, it is the gift of God—not by works, so that no one can boast. For we are God's handiwork, created in Christ Jesus to do good works, which God prepared in advance for us to do. (Eph. 2:8–10)

If you declare with your mouth, "Jesus is Lord," and believe in your heart that God raised him from the dead, you will be saved. For it is with your heart that you believe and are justified, and it is with your mouth that you profess your faith and are saved. (Rom. 10:9–10)

Once your Muslim friend begins to realize he needs Jesus the Savior, share the following verses in your Bible, as opportunity affords:

- Jesus is sinless (Heb. 4:15).
- Jesus is the High Priest (Heb. 7:24–25).
- Jesus is the perfect sacrifice (Heb. 9:13–14).
- Jesus is the healer (Matt. 4:23).
- Jesus is the Bread of Life (John 6:35).
- Jesus is the new covenant (Luke 22:20).

The Injeel proclaims that Jesus the son of Mary is the Savior of the world (John 4:42). He is called the Messiah, for he came to fulfill all the prophecies that a Savior would come.

The Bible clearly claims that *only* Jesus saves. Therefore, regardless of all the righteous acts we do on earth, none of us is righteous enough in God's sight. We might *feel* that we are more religious or pious than someone else, but we still fall far short of God's commands. We might *feel* that our actions are better than those of the terrorists, but we still fail to fulfill the law of God. His law is perfect; the standard we must measure ourselves against is perfection (James 2:10).

The Injeel claims that Jesus *alone* is the mediator between a holy God and a sinful humanity (1 Tim. 2:5). No sinner can have communion with a holy God; only Jesus can, for he is the Holy One, our redeemer and guide. Christ was sent so that we can receive forgiveness, experience power over sin, and see a perfect example of how to live.

If you observed a delicious meal, you could enjoy the sight and smell of it, but it couldn't nourish your body unless you took a bite. As we talk with our Muslim friends, it's essential to move the conversation toward their need to receive Christ as Savior and Lord. It isn't enough to hear the truth about Jesus, to gather some new information about him. Interest is not enough; commitment is required. Let's invite them to take Jesus as the Savior.

Read Revelation 3:20 and ask your friend if she would like to receive Jesus as Savior and Lord. If she says yes, then lead her in a prayer of commitment. The following might help:

> *Almighty God, I have sinned against you, and my sins are heavy on me. I repent of my sin and self-righteous attitude. I ask for forgiveness because of what the Messiah has done on the cross. I believe in my heart that Christ was raised from the dead. I commit to follow him as my Lord and Savior. I will follow your commands in the Injeel until my last breath. Amen.*

If your Muslim friend is hesitant, ask what one thing is holding her back from taking Jesus as Savior. You might need to address one of the hurdles and frustrations mentioned in this book. Or maybe there are other issues. Pray for your friend. Show your love and offer to help, if you can. Let us always be a people of compassion.

After I preached at a church in New Jersey, a Sunni couple came to the front. They told me they were having dreams of Jesus.

I asked, "How do you know it's Jesus in your dreams?"

"It's Jesus, the son of Mary."

"If you're sure it's Jesus appearing in these dreams, then what is your question?"

"Our question is, why is Jesus appearing in our dreams?"

I turned to Revelation 3:20 (ESV) and read it aloud with them: "Behold, I stand at the door and knock. If anyone hears my voice and opens the door, I will come in to him and eat with him, and he with me."

That day, it was my privilege to lead them in the prayer of salvation.

55 Seconds for Change

Here are several powerful Bible verses that proclaim Jesus to be the Savior of the world:

- John 3:16
- John 4:42
- John 8:24
- Romans 6:23
- Romans 10:13
- 1 Timothy 1:15
- 1 John 4:14

Memorize one each day of this coming week, and have them ready to share with your Muslim friends.

Part 4

A STRATEGY FOR
DISCIPLESHIP

Chapter 24

DISCIPLESHIP BASICS

Youssef, a young believer from a Sunni background, was attending a Bible study. As he studied the book of Acts intently, he sensed God calling him to reach out to others, just as God had called Paul. This young man said to me, "God told me, 'Rise up! I have a job for you.'" I was blessed to see a young believer moving toward maturity in Christ. This is the goal of discipleship.

Sharing the gospel and seeing people turn from darkness to light (Acts 26:18) is indispensable in doing evangelism. But our responsibility doesn't end there. Always remember that discipling new believers is foundational in fulfilling the Great Commission. The command in Matthew 28:19 is to make *disciples*—neither attenders nor acknowledgers—those who will obey *all* that Jesus commanded. This book would not be complete without touching on basic strategies for discipleship.

DISCIPLESHIP NECESSITIES

As you begin to disciple a new Muslim-background believer, here are a few things they'll need most. These points should help you move any new believer toward Christian maturity.

Time

New believers need your time. Make room in your schedule to visit them and listen to them. Time is easily wasted. So make an effort to see young believers regularly in a setting where they can share their feelings and ideas.

Hospitality

Make your time with new believers relaxed and hospitable. It can be over a meal at your home or in your friend's home; it might be going to an ethnic restaurant or function. It might involve sports or even shopping. Make room in your schedule to see them in a setting that isn't religious.

Small-Group Community

New believers don't need to be superstars. They don't need to be the center of attention. Many would prefer to remain low-key, lest there's persecution. They need a healthy community around them. Make sure the group is welcoming and cross-generational. Interacting with a multicultural, cross-generational group will enhance their spiritual growth tremendously as they meet and are blessed by Christians in different stages of Christian maturity.

TOPICS OF STUDY

As you meet with new believers, it's wise to have a strategy for discipleship. What follow are my recommendations for topics of study, but let God lead you and give you discernment. Make sure your study covers a specific topic related to Christian faith or a book of the Bible. If there is no goal, you'll have no direction to your study. New believers need to grow in their knowledge and character, and specific areas of study and discussion will help them do that.

An important note of caution: Make sure your time with new believers is focused on *them*. Don't let the study overshadow their lives and thoughts. On some days, you may need to stop and deal with an expressed deep need rather than to rush through an entire Bible passage that you worked hard to prepare. Be flexible, moving at the pace and needs of your friend. Always remember that you are an ambassador of Christ. It is God who transforms lives, not us.

The following is a suggested outline of six spiritual maturity discussions to be included in the discipleship process. There are many Bible studies that take up these topics. Or you can use a concordance or study Bible to look up Bible verses and passages that relate. I have suggested some here, but there are many more. For each discussion, you might want to try the inductive Bible study method:

- *Observe:* What is the passage saying?
- *Interpret:* What does it mean?
- *Apply:* What am I to do about it?

Another way to get the most out of your time studying God's Word together is to use Martin Luther's garland of four strands:

- *Instruction:* What is God teaching me in this passage?
- *Thanksgiving:* What am I grateful for?

- **Confession:** What do I need to ask God's forgiveness for?
- **Intercession:** What do I need to pray for?

Here is my discipleship outline to get you started. Feel free to adapt it according to your needs.

1. **Salvation Is a Gift of Grace**
   a. God's Character Is Agape Love—1 John 4:7–10
   b. Sin and God's Character—Habakkuk 1:13
   c. God's Plan for Salvation—John 3:16–18
   d. Jesus as the Redeemer—1 Corinthians 1:30
   e. Following Jesus—Luke 9:23–24; Ephesians 2:8–10; Revelation 3:20

2. **The Assurance of Salvation**
   a. Salvation Is a Free Gift—Romans 6:23
   b. Sacrifice and Atonement—Hebrews 9:22; 1 John 2:1–2
   c. New Creation—2 Corinthians 5:17
   d. God's Promises—2 Corinthians 1:20
   e. God's Faithfulness—Hebrews 13:5

3. **The Ministry of the Holy Spirit**
   a. The Holy Spirit—Genesis 1:2; John 14:16; 1 Corinthians 6:19–20
   b. The Role of the Holy Spirit—John 14:26
   c. The Holy Spirit and Our Daily Walk—Romans 15:13; Galatians 5:16
   d. The Holy Spirit and Our Daily Witness—1 Corinthians 3:16

4. **Walking in the Spirit**
   a. Surrender and Commitment—Matthew 16:25–27
   b. Fruit of the Spirit—Galatians 5:22–23

COMMUNION AND BAPTISM

Our faith has sacraments. A sacrament is a sacred moment, a time set aside to focus on God. Why are sacraments important? What do they symbolize and accomplish? We need to explain these clearly to new believers. Here's a starter for helping your friend understand communion and baptism.

Communion

> *While they were eating, Jesus took bread, and when he had given thanks, he broke it and gave it to his disciples, saying, "Take it; this is my body."*

> *Then he took a cup, and when he had given thanks, he gave*
> *it to them, and they all drank from it.*
>
> *"This is my blood of the covenant, which is poured out for*
> *many," he said to them. "Truly I tell you, I will not drink again*
> *from the fruit of the vine until that day when I drink it new in*
> *the kingdom of God."*
>
> —MARK 14:22–25

Two thousand years ago, Jesus the Messiah had a final earthly meal with his disciples before his crucifixion. It was a Passover meal. Moses, by the command of God, instituted this meal for the Jewish community—a meal to help everyone remember that God Almighty is the Redeemer from slavery, sin, and oppression. It is a holy time for Jews, for it marks the beginning of the people of God as they escaped Egyptian bondage (see Exodus 12:1–20).

For Christians, Jesus's Passover meal with his disciples was the start of a new tradition, known as communion in some churches and the Lord's Supper in others. The Bible is clear that the early Christian community practiced it regularly. Two elements must be present. The bread is to be broken and shared, and the cup is passed and also shared. One isn't to partake unless a believer in the redemptive work of Christ (1 Cor. 11:23–32).

How often should we partake in the Lord's Supper? There is no set time; the command is to do this in remembrance of Jesus's death and resurrection (Luke 22:19). Anytime Christians gather, they may partake.

Tell new believers how to receive the elements, explaining the meaning behind them. It's imperative that they see the Lord's Supper as a time of reflection, thanksgiving, and communion with other believers.

Communion isn't to be done to earn merit or favor with God. Neither is it to be done in a ritualistic manner, mechanistically going through the motions. Jesus instituted the act as a special moment when all Christians remember together the work of his redemption.

The word *sacrament* comes from the Latin word *sacrare*, which means "to consecrate."[16] When we partake of the Lord's Supper, we are acting on the outside while reflecting a reality on the inside: our redemption.

Experience communion with your friends who are new believers. The rich spiritual meaning behind communion will continue to ignite in them the joy of knowing we've been redeemed. One of my greatest joys in serving with Crescent Project is sharing in the Lord's Supper with Muslim-background believers from many nations.

Baptism

> *Jesus came from Galilee to the Jordan to be baptized by John. But John tried to deter him, saying, "I need to be baptized by you, and do you come to me?"*
>
> *Jesus replied, "Let it be so now; it is proper for us to do this to fulfill all righteousness." Then John consented.*
>
> *As soon as Jesus was baptized, he went up out of the water. At that moment heaven was opened, and he saw the Spirit of God descending like a dove and alighting on him. And a voice from heaven said, "This is my Son, whom I love; with him I am well pleased."*
>
> —MATTHEW 3:13–17

Baptism is, as with the Lord's Supper, a visible sign declaring on the outside what has taken place on the inside. Baptism comes from the word *immersed*.[17] It is an outward sign that a person has died to his former behavior and convictions. Now in Christ he enjoys a new life of redemption. "Those who accepted his message were baptized, and about three thousand were added to their number that day" (Acts 2:41). Baptism was an ancient sign of commitment.

> Don't you know that all of us who were baptized into Christ Jesus were baptized into his death? We were therefore buried with him through baptism into death in order that, just as Christ was raised from the dead through the glory of the Father, we too may live a new life.
>
> For if we have been united with him in a death like his, we will certainly also be united with him in a resurrection like his. (Rom. 6:3–5)

Baptism isn't to be taken lightly, for it's a symbol of a changed life. It's not a ritual to be repeated at the whim of some religious leader. Baptism is a sacred moment during which a follower of Jesus testifies that she is dead to sin and raised to life through the Savior Jesus. Its goal is to testify to others that she no longer belongs to the world; now she belongs to Jesus.

Baptism is a public proclamation, as Acts 2 indicates. This sacrament has special challenges for Muslim-background believers, but there are ways to deal with them. Many Muslims face severe persecution and increased harassment once that step is taken in public. Many choose to be baptized in secret, with a small group of witnesses and friends. Even in the generation that cares for stopping hate, many former Muslims who are now followers of Christ face hate, violence, and discrimination.

I have had the amazing privilege of baptizing my children

and many others who have decided to follow Jesus. There's unspeakable joy in seeing a redeemed person take a public stand for Jesus the Messiah. May the Lord use you in leading Muslims and others to faith in Christ and give you joy as you witness them emerge from the waters of baptism.

55 Seconds for Change

Read Acts 2:42-47. From your knowledge of people from Muslim backgrounds, what aspects of the early church would be especially appealing to them? How might you introduce them to these aspects of your faith?

Chapter 25

CONNECTING WITH A COMMUNITY

M embers of a Christian family in the United States con-tacted me several years ago, filled with excitement. They had befriended a Muslim family living across the street from them. How had this wonderful development happened? The Christian family members had invited their neighbors to share Thanksgiving dinner with them. And the friendship continues to grow. The Muslim family is now reading the New Testament and attending church. Why? Because they were attracted by the love of Jesus through a meal at a Christian home. They had experienced Christian community.

THE BODY OF BELIEVERS

The Bible discusses church as a *community*, not a building. The community of Jesus was called "the church"—in Greek, *ekklesia*, which means "assembly" or "the gathering."[18] It was understood to be a fellowship of those taking a stand against the norm.

The church is made up of those who aren't following the crowd but following Jesus.

The Scripture compares the church to a body of different parts, yet functioning as one unit: "You are the body of Christ, and each one of you is a part of it. And God has placed in the church first of all apostles, second prophets, third teachers, then miracles, then gifts of healing, of helping, of guidance, and of different kinds of tongues. Are all apostles? Are all prophets? Are all teachers? Do all work miracles? Do all have gifts of healing? Do all speak in tongues? Do all interpret?" (1 Cor. 12:27–30).

I appreciate this image of the body, for it helps us understand the purpose of community. Church isn't a political structure or even a club. We belong to Jesus, all together, and we're part of his body in this world in this time—his hands and feet, helping others.

The book of Acts also shows that the church of Jesus was made of different people and races (Acts 2:5–13), spreading from home to home (Acts 2:46). Therefore, we don't seek a physical building but rather a community of people. "From Attalia they sailed back to Antioch, where they had been committed to the grace of God for the work they had now completed. On arriving there, they gathered the church together and reported all that God had done through them and how he had opened a door of faith to the Gentiles. And they stayed there a long time with the disciples" (Acts 14:26–28).

This decentralized understanding of community differs greatly from Islam, which focuses very much on location. Muslims must have a formal mosque to fulfill their religious duties. While Christians are encouraged to gather together (Heb. 10:25) and assured that when they do, Christ is in their midst (Matt. 18:20). Communities are made of individuals, to change a society. You must change the individual; therefore, individual spiritual transformations happen best within a community. Our new Muslim-background disciples must see the value of being part of a *group*, even if it's a house church or a small group, rather than seeing the church simply as a building.

THE HALLMARKS OF A BIBLICAL CHURCH

A biblical picture of church is seen in Acts 2:42: "They devoted themselves to the apostles' teaching and to fellowship, to the breaking of bread and to prayer." New believers need to understand the true purpose of church if they are to grow into well-rounded, fruitful disciples.

The church must be *Bible-based*, following the teachings of Christ. Any church a believer considers joining must follow the Bible, not traditions or personality cults. Study and application of the Bible are how new believers grow, much like milk nourishes newborn babies. Young believers must lay a good foundation for their faith with an in-depth study of the Word of God.

Another hallmark of a solid, biblical church is *fellowship*. Because God has united us to himself through faith in Jesus by the Spirit, we have a filial relationship, giving us communion with one another as Christian brothers and sisters. Our experienced unity in Christ is fellowship.

Healthy churches *break bread*, or share meals, together. This isn't a rule to eat together a certain number of times per week but a recognition that we are members of the same spiritual family who will naturally look for ways to share our lives as we rejoice together in God's goodness.

Another key element of Christian community is *prayer.* Biblical prayer is simply having a conversation with God. It isn't wishful thinking, or repetitious statements in Arabic or any other language. It's engaging in heartfelt conversation with our heavenly Father. The Bible has outstanding examples of conversational prayer (Dan. 9:1–19; Hab. 1–2; Luke 11:2–5; Acts 9:11–16; Acts 10:13–15). A church that prays can empower new believers in their walk with Christ.

An Afghan believer I knew attended a church where her prayer life was encouraged, and many in the church prayed for her family. A year later, this woman's sister became a believer in Jesus. Now she and her sister are praying for the rest of their family.

Ideally, a church will be *diverse and will cross social barriers,* as demonstrated in the following passage:

Now in the church at Antioch there were prophets and teachers: Barnabas, Simeon called Niger, Lucius of Cyrene, Manaen (who had been brought up with Herod the tetrarch) and Saul. While they were worshiping the Lord and fasting, the Holy Spirit said, "Set apart for me Barnabas and Saul for the work to which I have called them." So after they had fasted and prayed, they placed their hands on them and sent them off.

The two of them, sent on their way by the Holy Spirit, went down to Seleucia and sailed from there to Cyprus. When they arrived at Salamis, they proclaimed the word of God in the Jewish synagogues. John was with them as their helper. (Acts 13:1–5)

The church in Antioch was multiethnic and functioning together, with members using their differences to create spiritual strength. The leadership included Africans, Europeans, and Asians. The church was also multicultural—gentiles, Jews, Greeks, and Africans all in leadership and praying together.

This church also *crossed barriers of social status and perception* to include leaders from all walks of life: politicians, traders, Roman citizens, and aristocrats. All were saved, worshiping and leading together. A church fellowship like this will help young believers learn to overcome their natural prejudices and love other cultures and peoples. It will help them see that God's salvation is for all ethnicities and cultures (Matt. 28:19). These gracious kinds of communities have helped countless new believers to grow in their Great Commission awareness.

Muslim-background believers, like all Christians, grow in their faith as they *share the gospel* with others. Even though sharing among family and friends might be hard for some of them, sharing the good news in another city or another part of town will help them grow in faith in a way few other activities can. Give them opportunities to do so.

Ali was a Shia-background believer in Jesus who served on a mission trip with our ministry. His testimony to Muslims in another nation was powerful and compelling. God uses each of our backgrounds—Muslim or non-Muslim—when we obey his Great Commission.

I pray that as you share with Muslims and they become believers, you will invite them to a church that meets the foundational criteria mentioned in this chapter. Muslims will not thrive spiritually if they don't join growing and vibrant communities of believers. The church is our hope to change lives and thus our cities, countries, and world.

55 Seconds for Change

Look again at the hallmarks of a biblical church highlighted in this chapter. How many of them characterize *your* church? How could you help your church grow in one or two of these areas? Jot down your ideas and make them a subject of prayer.

Chapter 26

POTENTIAL PITFALLS

An imam who had been baptized into the Christian faith was struggling because he had been deceived for so long. For years he had been taught falsehoods about the Savior Jesus, and he felt angry that this had gone on for so long. Another Muslim-background believer, a woman, was also seething. Starting at age seven, she had been directed to wear the hijab. Later, she had discovered that the hijab isn't even mentioned in the Qur'an.

Such anger is fairly common, but it is far from the only spiritual pitfall that new believers coming out of Islam may face. This chapter will look at this pitfall and several others. Our new brothers and sisters in the faith must be taught how to set up guardrails to protect themselves from unnecessary dangers in their Christian walk. These guardrails will help them maintain a God-focused lifestyle as they mature in their faith.

The Bible admonishes *all* believers to be on guard, not just those from Muslim backgrounds. We are to stand on the promises of God and live in his power, not ours. Paul told Timothy, "What you heard from me, keep as the pattern of sound teaching, with faith and love in Christ Jesus. Guard the good deposit that was entrusted to you—guard it with the help of the Holy Spirit who lives in us" (2 Tim. 1:13–14).

Notice Paul's use of the word *guard* as he wrote to his protégé, Timothy. God clearly is the one who protects us. The text also commands us to be on guard from pitfalls that damage our Christian life. Jesus made this clear in Matthew 16:6: "Be careful. . . . Be on your guard against the yeast of the Pharisees and Sadducees." The Pharisees and Sadducees taught a salvation achieved by human works. Against this pitfall Jesus warns us to turn not to the right or the left but instead to stay on the straight path.

Again, Paul cautions, "Timothy, guard what has been entrusted to your care. Turn away from godless chatter and the opposing ideas of what is falsely called knowledge, which some have professed and in so doing have departed from the faith" (1 Tim. 6:20–21).

Pitfalls don't necessarily take us off the road, but they do slow us down and create distractions on the journey. The following are spiritual pitfalls that we need to help new believers avoid.

BITTERNESS AND ANGER

Many Muslim-background believers feel bitter toward Islam and even Muslim people. Many say to me, "Once we discovered the truth about Jesus, we've become angry that our religious leaders lied to us all these years." Whether they were practicing Muslims or just nominal in their beliefs prior to salvation, their emotional hang-ups are understandable.

But this anger is a pitfall because it hampers their witness to Muslims and to other believers—and also because it harms them spiritually. You may have heard the common saying, "Resentment is like drinking poison and waiting for the other person to die."

So we must remind these friends what God says about forgiveness and of the hope that is ours in the gospel. An Afghan woman once told me how the bitterness of former Muslims toward Islam initially hindered her from considering Jesus's teachings. Only after she read Nabeel Qureshi's book *Seeking Allah, Finding Jesus* did she begin to identify with the language of love and peace.

SPIRITUAL PRIDE

Even the most dedicated followers of God, like Uzziah, can stumble on the path through pride, despite years of fruitful service (see 2 Chron. 26:19–22). Guarding against spiritual pride is difficult but not impossible. A young man I know, Ali Reza, embodies the kind of humility we need. When he became a believer about five years ago, he refused to make a public show of it. Knowing he was young in the faith, he simply focused on studying God's Word. Ali also made himself accountable to a strong discipleship group under mature leadership. What a joy to see him now amid fruitful ministry!

FEAR AND PERSECUTION

Fear of situations, people, or ideas can make new believers stagnate spiritually. With persecution so apparent in some Muslim communities, such fears can cripple the lives of new believers. Many Muslim leaders know how to stoke this fear.

Therefore, we must encourage young believers and surround them with prayer, building into them a biblical view concerning persecution and fear. Yes, persecution is always a real possibility for the believer (2 Tim. 3:12), but we never have to go it alone. Jesus said, "Do not be afraid" (Matt. 10:26). His reason? "I am with you" (Matt. 28:20).

After Ibrahim, a Sunni-background believer living in the USA, was baptized, his family got the local mosque to issue a fatwa that said he was a *murtad* (rejecter of his religion) and could lawfully be killed. Ibrahim responded to his natural fear by surrounding himself with people who pray regularly for his safety. Today he's walking in the power of the Spirit. His courage comes from Jesus, the risen Lord.

SHAME AND HONOR

The worldview of many Muslims today is colored by a strong sense of shame. Women in the Muslim world are shamed regularly, whether for their dress, their looks, their weight, their intelligence, or even the depth of their devotion. Carrying the shame and the honor of the family often becomes a woman's responsibility—a heavy burden indeed. For example, menstruating girls and women aren't allowed to fast and pray during Ramadan.

Yet from their childhoods men too must grapple with shame if they can't perform certain rituals in the accepted ways. The rituals of self-cleansing before prayer are exacting, and attempting to do them properly in the eyes of others can lead Muslim men into a kind of appeasement and performance anxiety. This attitude sometimes carries over when a Muslim becomes a Christian.

Of course, all of us struggle with pleasing and honoring others, but Christians know that the only honor we carry is the honor of the Savior. Jesus carried our shame (Isa. 49:7; Heb. 12:2) and gave us his honor, making us children of God (Gal. 3:26–29). What a liberating concept. Hallelujah, we have been redeemed! This truth is the only guardrail for the pitfall of shame. Muslim-background believers need to know they are held in honor by the King of Kings (John 17; Heb. 2:10). He loves them with an everlasting love (Jer. 31:3). They are his precious children (1 John 3:2), so there is no shame in his embrace.

Ali's mother always told him that he was worthless and would amount to nothing. Ali's shame drove him to honor his family any way he could. But after Ali found new life in Christ after reading the Bible and seeing a vision of Jesus, he was released from his shame. It no longer matters what his mother says about him, only what the Bible says, for Ali is a child of God.

Defeating the insidious power of shame is all about knowing the incredible love of God.

LACK OF CHURCH COMMUNITY

As noted in the previous chapter, Muslim-background believers usually must leave their Islamic communities when they follow Jesus. This is excruciatingly painful for most. Many Muslims I meet are deeply worried about offending the community. When Muslims come to Christ, it's like surgically removing their family and community life—and without anesthetic.

Sadly, former Muslims have often confided to me that the local church isn't welcoming. Feelings of inadequacy from the trauma of being rejected by their former community or immediate family may make it harder to join a church.

New believers must have a loving, supportive church community as they make the transition to a new life. So when you meet a Christian from a Muslim background, reach out with love. Be encouraging. Invite your new friend to dinner and into your home, building fellowship the same way the Christians of Acts 2 did. Remember that the community of Jesus really is the only hope for our planet.

55 Seconds for Change

Muslim-background believers dealing with anger, hurt, and bitterness over their former lives in Islam need to soak in the truths of forgiveness and hope. Here are some helpful verses you can share:

- *Forgiveness:* Isaiah 43:25-26; Ephesians 4:31-32; Colossians 3:13
- *Hope:* Jeremiah 29:11; 2 Corinthians 5:17; 1 Peter 1:3

Conclusion

REASON AND REVELATION

An imam in West Africa had a dream that made him doubt the Qur'an and seek a copy of the Book of Jesus (al-Injeel). Upon reading it, he compared its teachings with those of the Qur'an. God revealed the truth, and this man committed his life to spread the good news.

On a flight to the USA, a Shia businessman received a copy of the Bible. One year later he was baptized. The Word of God had convicted him.

A Sunni soccer player received an Arabic Bible as a gift and spent three years reading it and searching for the mistakes his Muslim teachers had assured him were there. But as this young man reasoned his way through the Word of God, he found faith instead of doubt and committed his life to follow the Savior.

A Sunni athlete had a conversation with a Christian lawyer who had been a Shia. Three months later, the Sunni became a follower of Jesus.

HOW DO MUSLIMS FIND GOD?

Throughout this book, an underlying question has been waiting quietly near the surface: Does God *reveal* the truth to Muslims, or do we have to *reason* with them for the truth? Do we just wait for God to send a dream or a vision for a Muslim to be saved? Or is it our daily role to reason for the truth of the gospel?

The answer to this important question is not either/or—it's both/and. God uses supernatural revelation *and* human reasoning to bring Muslims to Jesus. God is the one who calls us to this work. God uses our reasoning to show the uniqueness of Jesus, the validity of the Injeel, and the transforming power of the gospel. Jesus's final commission compels us to obey him. Our redemption brings so much joy that we *must* share it.

We bring our facts, testimonies, and apologetics to our Muslim friends, using the personalities and brain power that God gave us. These are the means that God appoints. But they are never enough, in themselves. Only God can close the deal and reveal himself to a Muslim heart—or *any* heart. As Ephesians 2:8 (ESV) declares, "By grace you have been saved through faith. And this is not your own doing; it is the gift of God."

You and I are like lamps, holding the light of Jesus high and inviting all to follow him. Yet we can compel no one. We reason, but God reveals. The Holy Spirit convicts all of us of our sinful state and places faith in our hearts (John 14:16–17; 16:8–11). Without God's supernatural work in the human heart, our best efforts will be to no avail.

From the dawn of creation, God has revealed himself. He reasoned with us through the prophets. Now more than ever, reason and revelation flow through this world, bringing God's lost children home and into his arms.

HIS AUTHORITY, OUR WITNESS

This book began with a detailed study of the Great Commission of our Lord and Messiah, Jesus of Nazareth. He has all authority on heaven and earth. It is on that authority that we move and speak and do his will, which is, that all will come to repentance (2 Peter 3:9).

Millions of Muslims are waiting for an authentic Christian witness. Many are dying through war, jihad, and terrorism. Many yearn to know a God who saves all people and loves all people. Sadly, in the last 1,400 years, more Muslims have died at the hands of other Muslims than at the hands of anyone else. Islam, whose adherents claim is a religion of peace, has failed to deliver true, lasting peace. Only Jesus can.

Jesus said he is the Good Shepherd, willing to leave the flock to search for lost ones (see Matt. 18:12–14; John 10:11). He said his sheep would recognize the voice of their Master (John 10:27). We see this truth before our eyes at this moment in history, as he brings unprecedented numbers from the Muslim faith into his fold. He told his disciples, "I have other sheep that are not of this sheep pen. I must bring them also. They too will listen to my voice, and there shall be one flock and one shepherd" (John 10:16).

Muslims are numbered among these "other sheep." Unfortunately, even after all the focus on the Muslim world in the last half-century due to the Iranian Revolution and the September 11 attacks, the harvest remains great, but the laborers are few (Matt. 9:35–38). One source estimates that only 4,200 Christian missionaries are focused on the over 1.7 billion Muslims living around the world. That's an average of only one missionary serving every 405,500 Muslims.[19] We simply don't have enough people willing and prepared to work among Muslims.

Some say Muslim hearts are hard. That may be true in some cases. But the bigger factor by far is the hard hearts of Christians who refuse to go to Muslims and share the good news. The need for proclamation is *urgent*. We are to share the gospel with all. Let us seize the moment and share the good news with every Muslim we meet.

As noted earlier in this book, in the last twenty years, God has surprised the Christian community with a new awakening in the Muslim world. God is revealing himself to Muslims more frequently than ever. Dreams and visions are part of this new movement of the Spirit, yes, but the Lord uses ordinary means too. One of them is authentic Christian friendships in which Muslims hear the gospel in nonthreatening and secure settings. Every day at Crescent Project, we see Muslims joining chat rooms and downloading Bibles and Christian literature.

Muslims are interested in Jesus, whom they know very little about. Muslims are asking about and investigating the claims of Jesus. Will we not help them? Let's boldly join God's work and partake of the joy of seeing people enter the kingdom. God is calling us to engage in a lifestyle of intentional living, focused on our matchless Messiah. Let's live in such a way that Muslims are attracted to our Savior.

Sometimes we Christians call interested non-Christians "seekers." Let me suggest that we *all* be seekers, for when we seek our Messiah, we will find him (Jer. 29:13). And so will our Muslim friends.

GLOSSARY

Abd Allah—A phrase meaning "Servant of God"; also the name of Muhammad's father.

abrogation—The doctrine held by some Muslims that certain teachings of the Qur'an have been repealed and replaced by later qur'anic revelations, opening the door to sanctioning violence against non-Muslims.

Ahmad—Muslims believe Jesus pointed to Muhammad as "most praised" or "commendable."

Ahmadiyah—An Islamic sect that believes Jesus swooned, rather than died, on the cross.

al-hudood—In Islam, guidelines or boundaries set by God.

Allah—The word for "God" in Arabic, also used by Muslims as the name of God in Islam.

al-Surat—In Islam, the road into heaven.

al-tawheed—"The oneness of God."

al-Wahid—A name for Allah meaning "the One" or "the only one."

assalamu alaikum—An Arabic greeting meaning "Peace be upon you."

Astaghfirullah—An Arabic expression meaning "God forbid!"

ayat—Qur'anic verses.

baraka—The blessings of Allah.

Bible—A book that includes the Tawrat, Zabur, and Injeel; the holy book of Christianity.

Christ—An English word from the Greek word *Christos*, meaning the Anointed One or the Messiah; one of the titles of Jesus.

dhimmi—A term describing Christians and Jews as inferior to Muslims.

eids—Arabic for "holidays."

fatwas—A compilation of legally binding teachings by Muslim leaders based on religious sources and documents.

five pillars—The creed (al-shahadah), the prayer (al-salat), the month of fasting (al-saum, or Ramadan), giving (al-zakat), and the pilgrimage to Mecca and Medina (al-hajj). They are incumbent upon every Muslim.

Gabriel—One of God's angels, mentioned in both the Qur'an and the Injeel.

God—The Almighty Creator of all that is and ever will be.

gospel—A word meaning "good news."

Hadith—An authoritative collection of stories about Muhammad's life, habits, and commands, compiled centuries later.

hajji—One who has accomplished hajj (see *five pillars*).

haram—Actions that are considered sinful or shameful.

hijab—Islamic apparel denoting that a woman is chaste and pure.

imam—A Muslim religious teacher.

Immanuel—Literally, "God with us"; one of the names of Jesus.

Injeel—The Arabic name of the Gospel of Jesus; an important book that Christians call the New Testament.

Isa bin Maryam—Arabic for "Jesus son of Mary"; one of the
   names of Jesus.

Islam—The religion of Muhammad and his followers,
   derived from the Arabic word *salama*, "to surrender."

Isma'il—Arabic name for Ishmael.

Jesus—The Messiah, an important figure in the Qur'an and
   the Injeel.

Jesus Christ—One of the names of Jesus; has the same
   meaning as "Jesus the Messiah."

jihad—Arabic word meaning "struggle"; can also mean holy war.

jinn, or genies—Half-human, half-demon beings, generally
   regarded as controlled by Satan.

jizya—A religious tax levied on non-Muslims cementing their
   inferior status.

Joseph—Husband of Mary, mother of Jesus; but not Jesus's
   biological father.

Ka'aba—The structure in Mecca housing the "Black Stone"
   meteorite, and around which Muslims march during
   the hajj (pilgrimage).

kafir—Arabic term for unbelieving people who reject the truth.

Kalimat Allah—The Word of God; one of the names of Jesus.

kuffar—In Islam, unbelievers.

madrasah—Religious schools that teach about Islam.

Mahdi—A spiritual and earthly leader who will, Muslims
   believe, restore religion and justice before the end of
   the world.

Marhaba—Arabic word meaning "hello" or "welcome."

Maryam—Arabic name for Mary, the mother of Jesus.

Masjid al-Haram—The world's largest mosque, in Mecca.

Messiah—A word meaning "Anointed One"; one of the
   names of Jesus.

mushrik—In Islam, a person who gives someone equal status with God; an idolater.

prophet—A messenger from God.

Psalms—Another name for the Zabur; songs.

Qur'an—Islam's holy book.

Ramadan—The Muslim holy month of fasting and feasting.

rasul—One who brings God's message.

ruh-u-llah—The spirit of God.

salam—An Arabic greeting meaning "peace."

shahada—The Muslim profession of belief.

sharia—Islamic religious law.

shirk—An act of idolatry.

Son of God—One of the names of Jesus.

Son of Mary—One of the names of Jesus.

surah—A division of the Qur'an; equivalent to a chapter.

Tawrat—The holy books of Moses; also called the Torah.

Ulul-azm—An Arabic Islamic term given to special messengers sent by God.

Word, the—One of the names of Jesus.

Yahya—John the Baptist, a prophet who told of Jesus's coming.

Zabur—The songs of David; also called the Psalms.

zebibah—A raisin-like mark on the head, caused by Muslim prayer.

NOTES

---

1. David Garrison, *A Wind in the House of Islam: How God Is Drawing Muslims around the World to Faith in Jesus Christ* (Monument, CO: WIGTake, 2014).
2. "42.7% of Muslims Illiterate, Reveals Census Data," *Wire*, September 1, 2016, https://thewire.in/education/census-literacy-religion.
3. "What Is Female Genital Mutilation? 7 Questions Answered," UNICEF, March 4, 2019, https://www.uniccf.org/stories/what-you-need-know-about-female-genital-mutilation.
4. "Bibles: Dangerous, Illegal, Covert," Love Packages, April 20, 2019, https://lovepackages.org/bibles-dangerous-illegal-covert/.
5. David Garrison in Lucinda Borkett-Jones, "We Are Living in the Midst of the Greatest Turning of Muslims to Christ in History," *Christian Today*, June 17, 2015, https://www.christiantoday.com/article/we-are-living-in-the-midst-of-the-greatest-turning-of-muslims-to-christ-in-history/56393.htm.
6. George Whitefield in Luke Tyerman, *The Life of the Rev. George Whitefield*, vol. 1 (New York: Randolph & Company, 1877), 328.

7. To learn more about them, you can reference my book *Ambassadors to Muslims* or go through a Bridges Study (www .bridgesstudy.com) through Crescent Project.

8. For more on this topic, please refer to my book *Ambassadors to Muslims*.

9. I previously shared a longer version of this outline in my book *Connecting with Jesus*.

10. *Life Application Study Bible: New International Version, Third Edition* (Wheaton, IL: Tyndale, 2019), 302.

11. For more information about the Trinity, see my book *Do Christians Worship Three Gods?*

12. This chapter contains material adapted from my book *Is the Injeel Corrupted?*

13. Sunan Ibn Majah, Book of Nikah, Hadith 1934.

14. "Progressive Revelation," Ligonier Ministries, May 24, 2016, https://www.ligonier.org/learn/devotionals/progressive -revelation/.

15. Garrison, *A Wind in the House of Islam*.

16. *Merriam-Webster*, s.v. "sacrament," accessed January 19, 2021, https://www.merriam-webster.com/dictionary/sacrament.

17. Blue Letter Bible, s.v. "*baptizō*," accessed December 17, 2021, https://www.blueletterbible.org/lang/lexicon/lexicon.cfm?t=kjv &strongs=g907.

18. Blue Letter Bible, s.v. "*ekklēsia*," accessed December 17, 2021, https://www.blueletterbible.org/lang/lexicon/lexicon.cfm?t=kjv &strongs=g1577.

19. "Missionaries and Workers," The Traveling Team, accessed December 17, 2021, http://www.thetravelingteam.org /missionaries-and-workers.